07908 246214

Bethel Daze

An Unadulterated Exposé of My Interactions with and Impressions of 27 Governing Body Members, and Other "Heavies"

Gary Alt

©2023 Good Leaf Publishing. All rights reserved. No part of this publication may be reproduced, distributed, or transmitted in any form or by any means, including photocopying, recording, or other electronic or mechanical methods, without the prior written permission of the author, except in the case of brief quotations embodied in critical reviews and certain other noncommercial uses permitted by copyright law.

ISBN: (print) 979-8-35090-006-4

ISBN: (eBook) 979-8-35090-007-1

To all who have escaped. To all who are escaping. To all those who may be waking up. To all who are making or have made something out of your lives with your freedom. To all those who are struggling. If even one of you gets some benefit from this book, it will have been worth writing it.

Table of Contents

PREFACE..1
Too Inquisitive For My Own Good..9
The "Truth...16
My First Circuit Overseer...20
The Absentee Circuit Overseer...28
Mister Moneybags Sends a Bethel Application.......................31
It's Who Ya Know, Ya Know......................................40
Breaking Bread With the Governing Body.............................46
Under the Rug...57
Saint George the Owl...64
SEX...74
The Umpire..81
Could It Be... Satan?...98
El Presidente..106
Opening Up..113
I Know Where You Live..118
Preserving the Sandbox...127
Shootout at the Fantasy Factory................................134
A Few Good Men...141
Hairy Carey..154
Mister Manners... er, Moneybags Again.........................171
Missed It By That Much...179
The Third Reich..188
Time to Go...200
Fun Facts..208
Why..212
GLOSSARY...216
INDEX..222

PREFACE

This book began its life in earnest about two years ago, in 2021. It was just an idea when, about ten years ago, someone had planted it in my brain to write about my experiences at Brooklyn Bethel, the USA branch and world headquarters of Jehovah's Witnesses. It seemed a cumbersome task with little point, until the thought of narrowing it down to writing about my interactions with and impressions of the Governing Body sprang up.

Work on this book had started and stopped so many times that I couldn't even count. Days of furious typing would give way to a period of doubts that these stories would interest or be of benefit to anyone. Another time of research and typing transpired, followed by another stretch of halting realization. While the chapters I had just created may be interesting and informative, there were still people to write about for whom I don't have much to say. And so it went, month after month, until December 2022.

At that time, the best stories were behind me, but there were still more to write if the end product was to include each man I actually knew and/or know, mostly personally but a few tangentially.

Then researching and typing recommenced, until I had everything but the conclusion and this preface.

The question still in my mind was, is this book necessary, or even desirable?

That question was answered when I reflected on how what I had written so far might help many who struggle with anger and resentment, frustration and powerlessness, over the effects of having been involved with Watchtower for much of their lives. Logically and in my heart, I knew that what was left to write needed to be completed.

What I have consistently observed among the post-JW community regarding the top brass at JW headquarters has made me realize that there is lot of healing that needs to take place in relation to organizational direction about teachings, behaviors, and punishments. There is an enormous amount of confusion as to where some of these things emanate from, and whether they are ubiquitous rules, or local phenomena peculiar to certain geographical areas, subsets of the overall JW community.

It can be likened to being attacked in the darkness of night by some unknown and unobservable intruder. If the trauma a person undergoes during such an experience is perceived as an attack from wild animals whose tame relatives may be household pets, the person may develop a morbid fear of all cats and dogs, including house pets, that will last their entire lifetime. If it can later be proven to the victim that the attack was not from that source, rather some other natural phenomenon was responsible, it may be possible to ameliorate if not eliminate the phobia.

When it comes to trauma experienced at the hands of the JW organization, a person may consider themselves completely free when they realize that activities and teachings of the organization no longer matter to them. They have moved on and are no longer concerned with JW goings-on, or what Watchtower and its adherents think about them. To get to that point, it is helpful, perhaps even necessary to understand the "enemy" at least to some extent and degree of accuracy. Once we have more accurate definition, we can more easily discard the organization from our hearts and minds.

It is not being suggested that if a person's experience is different from mine, and therefore different conclusions have been drawn, mine must be correct and the others incorrect. Such a viewpoint would be quintessentially arrogant. There may be truth in both viewpoints. It may be that the full truth of the matter lies at some as-yet unknown intersection of information. Therefore, please take these stories for what they are – my personal stories. They are 100% accurate, but they are by no means the entire story.

During this book's writing, it was discovered that by cross referencing historical documents with actual conversations between me and certain GB members, and between GB members and others mutually known, as well as information from Raymond Franz, accounts could be finalized and solid conclusions drawn as to their meaning and significance.

Good friends like Barbara Anderson, whom I overlapped with at Bethel for several years in the 1980s, as well as others also supplied certain invaluable information, and corroborated other information I already had but needed to confirm and flesh out.

What might surprise the reader is the juxtaposition of relatively positive stories about men whom I particularly loved, admired and respected, with others within the same circle that are/were less than admirable. Sometimes quite a bit less.

That is because my intent is to show all of these men as human, since they were and/or are. These stories should have the effect of taking the mystery out of an otherwise mysterious subject. Positive qualities and experiences are reported as such. The same is true of negative qualities and experiences.

Don't think for a minute that the good guys either did not see the bad guys for what they were, or saw but chose to ignore. In other words, "How can any GB member not be evil if he sits on the same body as so-and-so?" The fact that the good and bad co-existed is simply proof that the good guys sincerely believed in the supposed "truth" of the organization, and would continue to fight for it with every drop of their essence. Maybe we understandably won't see that as a good idea, but it does at least demonstrate good qualities, doesn't it?

We all have our own journey, including all of those depicted in this book. That should be understood and respected.

Most of the memories here are recalled fondly, some not so fondly, while a few others are very difficult for me to relate for personal reasons, and perhaps difficult for the reader for their own reasons.

I hope you can laugh at some things, as I choose to (in fact I can't help it at times). If some of it makes you angry, well, I can't say I blame you. Maybe you're not ready for this information yet. If that's the case, put it on the shelf for now. Read something else or talk to someone else you trust. Cry on someone's shoulder. Do what you have to do to get past whatever aspect of the process you are in.

A few rules of engagement.

Some terms will mostly appear throughout the book in acronym form, but the full expression will be used first. e.g. GB for Governing Body.

There will be a noticeable and consistent difference between the way males are referred to vs females. That is simply because all of the stories take place in an intensely patriarchal environment. It does not reflect any attitude or feeling toward gender groups, age groups, or authority figures on the part of the author. Where it is germane to the story to point out problems created by patriarchal views toward women, such will be noted. Otherwise all references are simply part of the story the way they actually exist(ed), therefore no judgment is intended.

Occasionally the term "heavy" may be used as a noun in connection with Bethel personnel, as in "So-and-So was a Bethel heavy." During my Bethel days, that word would refer to appointed men who carried a certain kind of prestige in the minds of Bethel family members. It's a rather nebulous designation that is based on a number of factors, some or all of which may be present in varying degrees. It's a perception thing, but the chances are that if one Bethelite viewed a certain man as a "heavy," most others would as well. I don't know whether the term is still in use.

When referring to people by name, the initial of a person's last name will usually be used if the person is not germane to the story.

The designations "brother" or "sister" will only be used if they are part of an actual quote. Otherwise, "husband," "wife," "woman," "man," and so on will be used.

When speaking about prominent men, either full names or last names will typically be used unless there is a reason to use a man's first name. That reason could be that the man was commonly referred to by his first name by many diverse people (e.g. Dan Sydlik), the author historically used the man's first name at times (e.g. George Gangas), and any other contextual considerations.

The standalone name "Franz" will always refer to Fred Franz, and Raymond Franz will be referred to either with his first name alone (Ray or Raymond), or both names (Ray Franz or Raymond Franz).

When referring to husbands and wives individually, use of the last name by itself will always be referring solely to the husband. (There is just one instance wherein I refer to a man's wife simply as "his wife." That is only because I'm not sure of the spelling of her first name, and although they were good friends at one time, there is no way for me, as an "out" person, to contact an "in" person for information.)

Too Inquisitive For My Own Good

Paradise. To a boy just arriving from the concrete jungle that was Brooklyn at the age of three, Westbury New York in 1962 was such a wonderland. Each house in the community of Levitt "slab" houses rested on what seemed like a vast oasis of lush green grass, with at least one pine tree in the front yard. By the time we moved there, a dozen years after thousands of acres of old potato fields became housing for the post-WWII baby boomer generation, our 60' x 130' lot also sported a cherry tree just outside the bedroom at the front of the house, and two apple trees, a pear tree, and a maple tree in the back yard.

That yard provided enough room for throwing and hitting baseballs, that is until my older brother Ed and I outgrew it to the point where we had to climb the next-door neighbor's rickety wooden fence to retrieve the ball nearly every time we made contact. At other times the yard served as an airfield, fulfilling Ed's primary passion (and my sometime casual interest) of building and flying U-control model airplanes.

I spent many summer days feeling like the king of the world perched on the upper branches of one of the apple trees that was perfect for climbing.

One of my fondest early memories of that property was the year that Dad turned it into an ice rink. He then hurled me, Ed, and my sisters Peggy and Patricia across it, one at a time, on garbage pail lids. It never occurred to me what skill it must have taken him to push us off with enough force for the ride of a lifetime, yet miss the fence belonging to the neighbors directly behind us. I guess I always just knew that whatever Dad did was done just right, and we would never get hurt if he was involved.

There were public baseball fields everywhere one looked in Westbury. The closest one to our West Cabot Lane house was a short walk from the Carman Avenue pool, another amenity of life on our part of Long Island just thirty miles east of Brooklyn Heights. All each family had to do was prove they lived in the neighborhood, and they got a pool tag for that year with no charge.

With all of those benefits, it never occurred to us four kids how little we actually had. There was only one car in the household, so in the days before we were old enough for Mom to leave us home alone for the twenty or so minutes it would take to drive Dad to the train station, he would have no choice but to drive himself, leaving us car-less. That was OK, since we only had to walk three blocks to get milk and other necessities at the deli, or other supplies at the nearby drug store – all on the side of Carman Avenue opposite that glorious pool!

We had a train set that was mostly a hand-me-down from my paternal grandfather, dating back to the early 20th century, and supplemented no more than once per year with new train cars, tracks, and even a Berkshire engine. We had a sled that served us well when we would sneak through the illegally cut chain-link fence to the storm basin at the end of our road (we called them "sumps"). Each of us had a bicycle, a rite of passage in those days. We went everywhere on our bicycles.

In later years, when all I could ever want was the new album by The Beatles, Jethro Tull, or my hero Eric Clapton, I was happy to get even just one of those, so long as the music and lyrics met my parents' standards. Nothing else mattered. How does a kid know how little he has when he has nothing to compare his circumstances to? Really, we had a lot. We even had a black and white TV that we could actually watch when the horizontal control wasn't having a complete conniption. Guess who we were watching on February 9th, 1964 on the Ed Sullivan show!

My parents were very conservative, including when it came to social fixtures like hair and clothing styles, entertainment, the friends we could have, and so on. I rarely had friends over, because it seemed like every time Dad got home from working in downtown Manhattan, New York City all day, he would figure out exactly what we were doing during the day. I swore it must have been that he had inexplicable magic powers. But alas, there was no magic wand to wave to get out of the punishment that might come our way.

There were two families on the block we were not allowed to associate with, and others that were always creeping up toward to the top of that same list of banned people. In hindsight, there were good reasons for that. But we couldn't understand it at the time.

Saturday mornings were often frustrating, since all we really wanted to do was stay home and watch cartoons. The man who spent over twelve hours each weekday commuting and working had other things in mind for us when we finally got to see him on the weekends.

At one point Dad bought a barber kit from Sears in order to save money on haircuts for us boys. I hated the short bowl cuts he gave us so much that I swear haircut days were the worse times of my life (up to that point). After all, by the time I was ten years old, long hair was a necessity if a boy expected to be perceived as cool.

Even though lots of kids at school wore "rough play" clothes to school, we were not allowed. I always had to be the nerd with the casual-but-neat trousers, the button down shirt, and the weird shoes that seemed to be designed only for St Stephen's

Lutheran church, where Mom dragged us to Sunday school every week. Another thing I hated. At least we had a laugh explaining all the things we DIDN'T learn, describing the goody-two-shoes twin sisters with the white, lacy, perfect clothes and matching Bibles they never unzipped, and sarcastically pining for the day when we might be allowed to use scissors to complement the construction paper, crayons and paste we played with there.

The Lutheran church was selected by Mom as a compromise between her Baptist background and Dad's Catholic background. To my knowledge, Dad never saw the inside of a church unless it was for a baptism, wedding or funeral. But somehow it mattered that we not be brought up Baptist.

Arrival at the grand old age of fifteen brings with it a certain amount of wisdom, experience, and depth. At least according to the one who is fifteen.

By the summer of 1974, I had finally got to see my hero, Eric Clapton, play live at the Nassau Coliseum in support of his new album, *461 Ocean Boulevard.* Stephen King had just published his first novel, *Carrie.* Mel Brooks' *Blazing Saddles* was still playing in the movie theaters. PBS television began broadcasting *Monty Python's Flying Circus*. I had gone to my first concert, Hot Tuna, late in the prior year – unaccompanied and with a ticket I had bought with my own paper-route money.

But there were other developments that were increasingly disturbing to me.

The United States had just crept out of the 1973 energy crisis.

India successfully detonated its first nuclear bomb, joining the club that had up until then consisted exclusively of the United States, Great Britain, the Soviet Union, China, and France.

The news was ever more frequently saturated with reports of terrorist attacks on England by the Irish Republican Army.

The US Senate Select Committee on Presidential Campaign Activities, having been convoked as a result of the break-in at the Watergate Hotel in Washington DC in 1972, carried out televised hearings during the summer of 1973. The committee finally published its Report on Presidential Campaign Activities on June 27th, 1974. President Nixon would subsequently announce his resignation on August 8th, effective the following day.

It felt like my country and the whole world were falling apart.

I had observed enough of children starving in Biafra, developments in Viet Nam, the Watergate scandal, and other country- and world-wide events, to wonder about the purpose of life. Add to that the fact that seemingly every December there were news stories of some family's house, along with all of the Christmas presents inside, burning to the ground in a fire usually caused by a badly decorated Christmas tree. For several years leading up to 1974 I didn't see much point in celebrating Christmas. How was I supposed to be happy getting more sleds, bicycles, and music records when there were kids somewhere that weren't going to get ANYTHING?

Obviously, the wisdom and knowledge I had gained up to that point did not include the art of seeing the positive things in the world, as opposed to seeing things through the bleak lens presented by network TV news.

I began wondering about the future. The purpose of life. Having recently read Dante's *Inferno,* I wondered about the condition of the dead.

There were no answers at the Baptist church Mom finally began bringing me to when I was thirteen or fourteen years old.

Would I ever get those answers anywhere?

The "Truth" That Leads... Nowhere

Charlie D and I had known each other since the age of three, when I had just moved to Westbury. His house sat catty-cornered from ours, the two properties sharing a border of just about ten feet. I could either walk around the block to his house in about five minutes, or squeeze between the fences and into his back yard to be there in a fraction of that time.

Our friendship was on and off for years. We attended the same class throughout most of elementary school, and of course went to the same high school, although we were almost never in the same classes in high school.

By the summer of 1974, we were once again friends. Best friends. So tight that I don't think there has ever been a more intense friendship. Kids in school would even sometimes remark about how inseparable we were. We did everything together. All day, every day, especially during summer.

What I never knew was that Charlie's mother had become one of Jehovah's Witnesses when he was four or five years old. I always noticed how he appeared to be a clean-cut, good and respectful kid, but at the same time he had an edge to him that was hard to define. I was always expecting him to catch hell for doing something wrong in school or elsewhere, but it seemed that he never did. Since I had never heard of Jehovah's Witnesses up to that point, he seemed to be a living paradox, created by a religion he wanted no part of. He had no choice about the matter.

One summer day in 1974, when Charlie and I were customarily hanging out, doing nothing, he asked me if I wanted to go on a Bible study with him.

Charlie informed me, "I have to go somewhere. I can't hang out with you today."

"What? Are you kidding? What do you have to do?" (It seemed to me that some terrible injustice was taking place.)

"I study the Bible with a girl from Hicksville. Do you want to come with me?"

I hesitated for just a brief moment. Then I expressed surprise that he didn't just HAVE a Bible, he actually STUDIED it. And HE was the TEACHER?? Then I agreed.

"Sure. When, now? … Where in Hicksville?"

"Yeah, in a few minutes ... Just the other side of Wantagh

Parkway off of Rim Lane. So we can walk there."

Charlie was sixteen years old, and his student, Rose M, had recently turned fifteen, being just four months younger than me. Her friend, Delores K, also sat in on the study.

They were studying *The Truth That Leads to Eternal Life,* the book that I came to know as the "Blue Bombshell."

By the end of that study, I had learned at least three Hebrew words and three Greek words. For the first time I had a then-satisfying explanation about what hell is, what the condition of the dead is, and what hope there is for them. I felt a sense of exhilarating liberation that I could not even describe. God was beginning to be a real person with a name that I could come to know.

Afterward, Charlie[1] asked me if I wanted to have my own Bible study. Of course I said Yes.

He and his mother, Sylvia, soon explained what the Kingdom Hall was, and asked if I wanted to attend a meeting. I did so that very Sunday.

I didn't get much out of the program. The speaker had a thick

---

1 Charlie finally left Watchtower at some point in his twenties. In his own words, "I found Jesus as my Lord and savior 30 years ago. I am a practicing Born Again Believer living under grace."

accent that I was unaccustomed to at that point in my life. And the 32-paragraph Watchtower study article was too dense for someone who hadn't seen a Watchtower before the moment the study started.

I became so bored that I decided to launch into my version of the phony cough that Ozzie Osbourne began the song *Sweet Leaf* with, on the Black Sabbath album *Master of Reality*. (The song is an ode to marijuana.) That provided comic relief for Charlie as well as a few high school friends that were scattered among the audience, all of us being Black Sabbath fans to one degree or another. What made it even funnier was their difficulty in trying to suppress their laughs.

It certainly wasn't the information that impressed me at that first meeting. It was the people, as well as the simplicity of the building compared with St Stephen's church. This boy, who had had very little association up to that point with anyone who wasn't of white, western European descent, was meeting people "of color" that were genuinely warm, welcoming, and just an absolute pleasure to be with. Also, I loved what I was learning from Charlie and Sylvia, and I knew it was connected to that Kingdom Hall.

On the way home, Sylvia explained to me that there is a special meeting coming up Tuesday night. It has to do with the visit of someone called a Circuit Overseer.

My First Circuit Overseer

There is no doubt that the stature of a Circuit Overseer, the aura he exudes, is directly proportional to the esteem in which his admirers hold him. When someone speaks glowingly of a person, the natural tendency of the listener, especially if he is young and impressionable, is to start with a deep but as-yet unearned respect for the person.

The first Circuit Overseer I ever met was Samuel Herd. Herd has been a member of the Governing Body (GB) since 1999. My first encounter with him was in 1974, at my second Kingdom Hall meeting.

Herd had an eloquence I was not accustomed to. It was a pleasure listening to him, not only due to his speaking ability and his engrossing subject, but because after a few Bible studies and one congregation meeting, I was already hooked. I loved going to the Kingdom Hall, meeting all of those wonderfully warm people, and soaking up all the new things that I found so exhilarating.

All these years later, I only remember two related features of

Herd's presentation. He spoke of examples of faith, and he spoke extensively of demons.

One of his stories was that of an elderly woman who went home after a meeting and discovered that there was an intruder hiding under her bed. Realizing that if she tried to run, her old body would not make it to the door safely, she decided to kneel down beside her bed and pray aloud. She could feel the man's breath on her knees as she asked God, whose name I had just learned recently, for his protection. The man subsequently bolted from underneath the bed and fled from the house, but not before inexplicably grabbing her Bible. Many months later he came face to face with her at a JW meeting and explained to her that he was the intruder that night, and that her prayer frightened yet moved him. He didn't know why he had grabbed her Bible, but it led him to studying with the JWs and he was now her "brother."

I was mesmerized.

What I neither realized nor understood was that from that very moment, fear was being used to indoctrinate me. According to Herd and JWs in general, this world is chock full of evil people looking to do bad things at every turn. Our "sister" had been at a meeting, as the good and obedient JW she was. She went into that "strong tower," using God's name. That alone protected her from evil. Otherwise she would have been robbed, raped, and/or killed.

Up until that day I had no belief in Satan or demons. Since then, I continued to have no experiences that would suggest that they exist. Yet on that night, I came to believe in them as realities to be avoided at all costs. Something to fear unless I obey God (READ: The people who taught me about them).

Outside in the parking lot I and a number of the congregation kids my age oohed and aahed about what a great talk it was. I was learning how to trust God. Or rather, I was learning how to irrationally fear everyone and everything that is not JW-associated, and only then would I experience trust in and protection by the God I was learning about.

It all started with Samuel Herd, an eventual GB member.

My only other recollection during those years is that he has a medical condition that prevents him from shaving his beard. The curly hairs grow back into his skin, causing infections and making it impossible to shave without a lot of cuts and bleeding. So he used (and perhaps still uses) a depilatory product to remove his beard every day. I believe the product he used at the time was Nair.

Interestingly, it is Samuel Herd who famously has given talks about women's physiology preventing them from having anything other than a subservient role to men. He has said, "Scientists say that the cranial capacity of a woman is 10% smaller than that of a man. This shows that she is just not equipped for the role of headship."

Herd neither said nor implied that all women are less intelligent than men. In fact, he went on to say that, "often times [it] is the case" that a wife may be "quicker of mind" than her husband. However, that does not mean that her superior intelligence should prompt her to "pit [her] mind against his." Rather, she should, "work extremely hard never to show that she's quicker of mind than her husband." (READ: Play dumb.) Somehow he went on to equate that competitive spirit with homosexuality. Then seemed to confuse homosexuality with transgenderism, although the latter term was not specifically used.

Herd's first two sentences present two distinct logical fallacies.

First, by referring to "scientists" in the first sentence of that particular section of his speech, Herd presents an argumentum ad verecundiam (appeal to authority, or argument from authority). Although he does not refer to any scientific study or paper, and even though no connection is made between his initial statement and the suppositions that follow, he is using scientific authority as proof of his correctness. It so happens that there is some truth to his statement about male vs female brain size, which will be discussed in a moment. However, he does nothing to verify that information – his audience is expected to believe it because of that magic word, "scientists."

Second, by drawing the conclusion that the initial reference to scientists "shows that [women are] just not equipped for the role of headship," he presents a propositional fallacy. A propositional fallacy is one that says, "If A is true, then B." There is no need to prove the correctness of B, it is just assumed because of A. For example, "The air in San Diego is cleaner than that of Los Angeles, therefore people in San Diego are healthier than that of Los Angeles." Even if a difference in health between the two peoples exists (B), it cannot be proved by A.

Most of the remainder of this section of his speech simply decays into more and more propositional fallacy.

Since Herd's sole scientific reference has to do only with cranial capacity, his argument completely ignores all other physiological factors that may affect brain function. Just one of many examples of such factors is the gender-specific production and activation levels of serotonin in the brain.

If all other factors are static (including male vs female

intelligence and leadership qualities), then brain size may be used to draw conclusions. Since those factors are variable, brain size alone cannot be conclusive.

Actual scientific studies have demonstrated that women's brains are in fact about 11% smaller than men's *in proportion to body size* - that italicized clause was not included in Herd's argument. Please note that body size takes into account height and overall frame (not weight).

The American Association for the Advancement of Science reports, "Smaller brains allow certain features, such as a slightly higher ratio of gray matter to white matter, and a higher ratio of connections between, versus within, cerebral hemispheres."

Gray matter is where the neurons that make connections associated with thinking and memory are made. White matter has a somewhat different function, that of transmitting signals between the brain and spinal cord and beyond. Does that mean that women actually have a cognitive advantage, since they typically have a higher ratio of gray vs white matter?

The left brain hemisphere is predominantly the logical side. It processes data, numbers, facts, but also language and rhythm. The right brain hemisphere is predominantly the creative side. It processes emotions and melody. Of course that is not the whole story, but it is generally true. Since women's brains typically form a higher ratio of connections BETWEEN hemispheres, that logically means that, on average, they are better at associating emotions with logic, melody with rhythm, creativity with facts and other data. Does that mean that the brain function of women, on average, is more efficient, more complete, or better than that of men?

Lisa Eliot, Professor of Neuroscience and Executive Chair of Foundational Sciences and Humanities at Rosalind Franklin University of Medicine and Science, says, "This [the relationship of brain size to height and frame] means that the *brain differences between large- and small-headed men are as great as the brain differences between the average man and woman*. And importantly, *none of these size-related differences can account for familiar behavioral differences between men and women*." [Italics mine]

Using Herd's logic, taller men should be more suited for headship than shorter men. Even if the taller man has suffered brain damage, was born with Fetal Alcohol Syndrome, or has an organic brain disorder that has left him with a greatly diminished IQ. It's all about brain size, if we are to agree with Herd, and taller men typically have greater brain size than shorter men.

However, even if a 6' woman has a larger brain than a 5' man, it is the man alone who is naturally equipped for headship, according to Herd. Because she is female, and, "Scientists say that the cranial capacity of a woman is 10% smaller than that of a man."

There is also a tacit implication that a single mother is not equipped to head her family, because she is a female with reduced cranial capacity.

What a shame. Herd has no business espousing anything he imagines may have to do with science. He evidently is not equipped for it.

Thankfully, I only heard one of those speeches since leaving the JW organization. Had I heard such when I was "in," I seriously doubt it would have had any impact on me, other than prompting an internal grimace and shake of my head. Perhaps because my own "cranial capacity" is sufficient to recognize and reject bullshit when I hear it.

The Absentee Circuit Overseer

"Thanks for your visit, it was lousy."

Bill W, one of our three elders in my early days in Westbury, said that to Theodore Jaracz.

The elders in Westbury were an unusual bunch. Never did they force their opinions on me or the congregation in general. They were fair, judicious and loving, and respected each member of the congregation they served. But if there was something constructive, albeit politically incorrect, to say to even the top JW brass, they were going to say it. (Two of them had a direct line with Harley Miller, who more or less WAS the Service Department in those days.) I would only learn years later that those qualities are somewhere between rare and nonexistent elsewhere in the organization.

What Bill W was complaining about was the fact that our congregation was being ill-served by a Circuit Overseer who barely managed to show up on Sunday, leaving most of his duties to a local substitute.

How did this situation develop?

Jaracz had spent five years as the branch overseer of the Australia branch starting in 1951. It was understood by some that he was a gay man. Over time, four young men had separately accused him of homosexual behavior toward them. He was returned to the United States, soon thereafter marrying Melita Lasko on December 10, 1956. It would seem that Watchtower President Nathan Knorr's solution to the gay question exerted sufficient pressure, since it was known that Jaracz did not want to marry. Jaracz' new situation in a part of the world far from where he had previously served had the effect of shifting talk from that of homosexuality, to that of a man and his wife selflessly immersed in Circuit and District work. They variously served in British Columbia and Pacific coastal United States. Any new accusations of homosexuality would not be taken seriously by the congregations in that part of the world.

In the early- to mid-1970s, thoughts of new appointments to the Governing Body combined with the realization that a man must be a Memorial partaker ("anointed") to be a candidate. Jaracz began partaking. In 1974, the year that Knorr invited him to Brooklyn Bethel, Lloyd Barry was also asked to become a member of the GB. Barry, having served in New Zealand and Japan for years, knew of Jaracz' spotty reputation. He voiced strong objections to Knorr about it and Jaracz' qualifications. Knorr's concession was to initially assign Jaracz to circuit work in Nassau County, Long Island, with my home town of Westbury being dead center. All the while he would live and work at Bethel.

Naturally, as a teenage boy, I knew nothing about any of this, except that he was our "part time" Circuit Overseer. He never generated any warm feelings in me, or anyone else for that matter. However, I do remember Jaracz' talks at the Circuit Assembly every half year or so. His perfect diction and eloquence left me quite impressed. Everything that rolled off his tongue seemed to make complete sense and be absolutely correct. Even though his body language exuded rigidity, he was a pleasure to listen to.

I came to know Ted and Melita personally during my time as a Brooklyn Bethelite in the early- to mid-1980s. More on that later. Suffice to say that I loved, admired and respected all of the fifteen GB members that I came to know at Bethel. To different degrees. Jaracz was my least favorite. By far. I believe I shared that feeling with most if not all of the Bethel "family."

Mister Moneybags Sends a Bethel Application

Sometime in the late 1970's, the Westbury body of elders began to grow. Not as fast as the congregation in general, but grow it did.

Gary S was a lawyer in his late twenties who had just been baptized before I began attending meetings. Soon after, Gary was appointed as a Ministerial Servant, and among other things, served as my Book Study Conductor. Not long after, he was appointed to the elder body. (He is now no longer one of Jehovah's Witnesses.)

He came to do legal work for Watchtower, eventually spending one day a week at Brooklyn Headquarters. He was the lawyer that closed their real estate deals for many years. He worked directly with people like George Couch (Bethel Home Overseer) and Grant Suiter (Secretary-Treasurer of the Watch Tower Bible and Tract Society of Pennsylvania and GB member).

Thanks in part to Gary, Westbury began to have more and more visits from Bethel luminaries. I will never forget a visit by now-GB "helper" Robert Wallen. In addition to the regular Sunday meeting, there was the customary Saturday-night special talk by the Bethel speaker. Wallen's subject was the tragic situation in Malawi. At the end of his extraordinary and deeply emotional discourse, he broke out in tears and his voice trembled when he said that, through all of the outrageously inhumane persecution, "not one of our brothers or sisters has given up or compromised."

I only learned the truth about the Malawi situation many years later. Thanks to a rule that says a motion made within the GB must have a 2/3 majority in order to carry, the faithful in Malawi got no relief from the GB. Yet that stance contradicted the GB's direction on a somewhat similar situation in Mexico. It was deemed acceptable for JW men in Mexico to bribe certain officials to falsify documents in order to make it appear as if they had completed mandatory military service, then carry on with life in a relatively carefree manner. It bothered the consciences of even many Mexican JW men, including branch members, that they were permitted to perform such bribery, all the while the faithful in Malawi were being mercilessly brutalized for not buying a party card that cost less than the equivalent of US$ 1. The GB did not change their stance on the situations in either Mexico or Malawi. The vote to bring relief to those in Malawi came up within the GB a number of times. At times there was a simple majority in favor of change, even falling just one vote short of the required 2/3 majority. The majority of the GB had voted for change, but it was not a 2/3 majority. So the carnage in Malawi that started in 1967 continued unabated until 1993, when the government finally lifted the ban on JW activities. In the late 1970s, like all JWs, I was completely ignorant about any of these facts. I did as everyone else – included the "brothers in Malawi" in my thoughts, prayers and comments, made it one of my personal proofs that I was "in the truth," allowed their sterling example to help build a stronger faith in me, and occasionally shed tears thinking about those dear people.

A few years later, we met two young Bethelites at a party at the home of someone in our congregation. Presley C and Dennis L played a game of Uno, listened to music, and shared some stories and laughs with all of the guests that included me and my then-wife.

We became friends with both of them, but especially Presley. While playing cards at the party at which me met, Presley for some reason said, "Accidents will happen." I responded, "But only hit and run," echoing the words from a recent Elvis Costello song. Presley instantly picked up on it, and we bonded over the fact that we were both Elvis fans. He became a frequent weekend guest of ours, and we sometimes visited him at Bethel. We were making stronger and stronger Bethel connections.

Sometime around 1979 or 1980 we spent a week in North Carolina visiting a couple we knew from both Westbury and Brooklyn – Larry M (a Bethelite from Tennessee) had married Marie S (from Westbury), and they moved to Beaufort, a town on North Carolina's beautiful Atlantic coast. There we met another couple with a Bethel connection – the husband had served there as a young man. They married and served together for a very short time at Bethel. She became pregnant, so they had to leave.

Our conversations with them were peppered with excitement and regrets about serving at and having to leave Bethel. That, combined with all that we were learning about Bethel from Presley, engendered in us a desire to serve there. By then I was a computer programmer, making steady advancement in my career. I began to realize that I could do much more for the world-wide work using those skills in the relatively new computer department at Bethel than I could ever do on the "outside." Working for Arrow Electronics (the second largest electronics distribution company in the United States) in Farmingdale New York seemed far less purposeful and meaningful to me.

During the trip home, we discussed it. My wife was willing to do ANYTHING that had to do with the "kingdom work," even become a Gilead Missionary, if that's what I wanted.

I knew that Grant Suiter was scheduled to be our Bethel speaker at the next meeting after we returned home. I decided to ask him a few things about Bethel.

I was careful to remain quite nonchalant when I met "Grant" well before the meeting, having arrived early enough to beat the crowd at the typically jammed, noisy Westbury Kingdom Hall. In those days I was in the habit of calling everyone by first name, including the elders and even celebrities like Suiter. I think I did that in order to appear older, more mature. If memory serves me, I said Hello to "Grant."

Other than that, I was suitably respectful, believe me. All right, don't believe me. Whatever.

Realizing he would soon be swamped by eager fans, I simply told him I had a question for him if and when he had time. He immediately grabbed me by the upper arm and pulled me to a more private spot a few feet away, and advised me to ask him anything I would like. My heart instantly swelled with love for this man, and I knew it would be a good conversation.

I told him I wanted to know whether I might qualify for Bethel – my wife was a pioneer, but I was nothing more than a working stiff – surely Bethel only accepted regular pioneers. I asked him if it was true that Bethel needed computer programmers.

As I would find out in just another year, Suiter was the brains behind Watchtower's shift to computer technology, an idea that met much opposition from the isolationists. He therefore was excited when I told him I was a programmer. He explained that in some cases, such as mine, pioneering is not necessarily a prerequisite for serving at Bethel.

By the end of the meeting we learned that Lisa H, elementary school aged daughter of our dear friends Adam and Joanne, was in the hospital. Gary made arrangements to visit her and brought Suiter along. Of course I tagged along also.

Adam knew Suiter from his days at Bethel about a decade previous. He was guardedly civil about greeting Suiter, at the same time appreciative of his willingness to visit them at Nassau County Medical Center.

The last thing I remember conversing about with Suiter there at the hospital was sealing up our desire to apply for Bethel. He said he would send me an application. And he did so. I received a Bethel application personally from Grant Suiter within a few days. I would later learn that he was the chairman of the Administrative Data Committee (ADC), which oversaw the work of the department I would land in. Hence I would come to know and work with him more intimately in not too long a time.

My elders felt broadsided by the whole thing, since they had no idea we were even thinking about Bethel service. But they were happy for us, and did everything they could to help.

Still, our Bethel application languished for about a year. The mantra is, "If we accept your application, you'll know when we invite you. If you're not invited, we either haven't decided yet or you're not going to be invited."

Helluva communication system for a job change from a $25,000 per year position (in 1980), to a few dollars and room and board. And for liquidating an entire household and moving it – for some people that move may be thousands of miles. Helluva system.

An interesting thing happened while we were still in Westbury, waiting for word on our Bethel application. For several years I had worked on the stage at District Conventions with the overseer, Monroe F, who was an elder in my congregation. I adjusted mics, set up tables and other props, and so on.

Grant Suiter was one of the speakers one day at Belmont Racetrack in Elmont New York. Monroe alerted me to the fact that Suiter would need a glass of water for his throat. It had to be a clear glass so that it was not visible to the audience (I guess that would otherwise be a problem?). I had about a half hour to spare. I ran from the stage to the grandstand and went from one end to the other trying to find, not just any ol' drinking vessel, but a real, clear glass. I finally found one in the last possible place. I just made it back to the stage in time for the afternoon session to start. Of course Suiter never knew about any of that, so no thanks were offered. I was still happy to have done it and considered it a great privilege.

Suiter's talk was delivered from a manuscript. That means he didn't write it. Someone in the Writing Department did. He just read it. I noticed one, and only one marking in his manuscript.

In a section that was talking about the so-called self-will so prominent in this world, and how we need to avoid that tendency, his script mentioned people's tendency to "do their own thing." Suiter changed that one phrase to, "go their own way."

Monroe also noticed that change as he followed along in his own copy of the manuscript. The conclusion we drew was that, "do their own thing" was viewed by Suiter as a modern colloquialism, smacking of the "world." He wasn't about to speak that way to his audience of 20,000 or more.

Anyone less than a GB member would likely get in trouble for altering the words that came down from the Writing Department. To GB member Suiter, those words came "up" to him from the Writing Department. He did what he wanted with them.

It's Who Ya Know, Ya Know

Presley was giving his first public talk in his congregation, Clason Point, Bronx, New York. We were invited. Ciro Aulicino, from the Writing Department, also attended with his wife Lolly.

After the meeting we were entertained by a family in the congregation. I conversed with Ciro about our Bethel application for which we had no updates in about a year. After asking me about my skill set, how long my wife had been pioneering, and so on, he said he had a friend in the Personnel Department whom he would call to have the application expedited.

The friend he was referring to was GB member Daniel Sydlik. Nearly everyone referred to him as Dan, so I will usually do so from this point on.

I don't know exactly how Ciro and Dan knew each other, apart from both being prominent members of the Bethel family[2]. But I do know that they were both on the Family Night Committee.

---

[2] Sydlik had also worked in the Writing Department for some time before being disciplined for plagiarizing a *Reader's Digest* article. He was then assigned to work in the factory, which he did right through his eventual appointment to the Governing Body in 1974. Soon thereafter he was transferred to an office job in the Personnel Department.

I would become a constant performer as a pianist on Family Night for all my time at Bethel, so I came to know those men quite well. But for now I just knew that Ciro was a nice guy, and that he knew Dan Sydlik personally. He was going to call Dan Sydlik. About me and my wife. Dan Sydlik. Dan The Man. No kidding.

Not long after that, I got a call from Ed Sainthill, overseer of the Computer Department. As overseer, he was responsible for all computer activities not only in Brooklyn, but Watchtower Farms as well. MEPS (Multilanguage Electronic Phototypesetting System) was being developed at the Farm, and the IBM-based phototypesetting system in Brooklyn (later called WatchText when they started selling it to outside companies). He wanted to meet with me, my wife, and three others from the computer department, Terry Poland[3], Darrel Christianson and Russell Fields. He explained that that is rarely if ever done, but since we lived only thirty miles away, it seemed prudent.

In those days the Computer Department was in the factory at 117 Adams Street; I don't recall which of the four buildings. That is where we met. I learned that, in addition to the

---

3   After leaving Bethel in the mid 1980s, I worked for Terry when he owned a software company in Wayne, New Jersey. Our job was to customize and enhance WatchText for companies that bought the software from Watchtower. The main company I worked with was Standard & Poor's. Later I worked with Reader's Digest before leaving for greener pastures.

Phototypesetting system, the Society had decided that they might as well use the IBM mainframe computer for a few business applications. The first one they chose was the Mortgage system for the Treasurer's Office (TO). The Mortgage system automated the management of mortgages and insurance for Kingdom Halls everywhere in the United States.

Soon thereafter they realized that they didn't want to tax the resources of the IBM mainframe with too many systems, so they invested in an IBM System 34, a much smaller computer that used a programming language called RPG II (Report Program Generator II). The System 34 would be the administrative systems computer. (By the time I joined the team the computer had been upgraded to a System 38, which used a significantly enhanced programming language called RPG III.)

A few weeks after our interview, I got a call from Sainthill informing us that they we were accepted. They would be calling us in.

What I didn't realize was that merely meant they were RECOMMENDING us to the Personnel Department (Sydlik's department). What Personnel would do and when they would do it was not for the little ad hoc committee in the Computer Department to know.

Meantime, I had called Sainthill to find out what the holdup was. Sometime after he informed me about the process, I then decided to call Personnel to get a REAL answer. I spoke with Sam Friend, who advised me to sit tight and let the Lord's work take place on its own terms, etc. Okay. I guess.

Eventually, sometime in early September 1981, we got a letter from Personnel inviting us to Bethel. We were to arrive on Friday, October 9th.

I was accustomed to informing my parents of every raise and promotion I ever got at work. I was the only one of their four children who was a JW, the only one to not go to college, and the only one to never need money from them. Because I was also the one who made the most money at that time, and the only one who had no school loans and related expenses to need help with.

I wanted them to know that I was doing well, hoping they would be proud of and happy for me. It was part of me "giving them a good witness."

Naturally the day would come when I would have to tell them

that I was leaving my then-current job to work as a volunteer, making $65 per month including travel expenses. I had just called them a few days prior to tell them about the raise that brought me up to $25,000 per year, the same salary as my father at the time. Now I had to call them to let them know that I was giving it up.

Their reaction was not good. They called my in-laws for support. My mother-in-law, a JW, fully supported us. My mother told her she was "one of them," and demanded she put her non-JW husband on the phone. My father-in-law then recommended they calm down, that the young couple had enough resilience to bounce back if this is a mistake.

Eventually my enormously frustrated parents got over it, at least to some extent, when they realized there would be no dissuading us. Keep this in mind as I talk more about my relationship with Dan Sydlik later in this book.

The death of my paternal grandfather led us to request a change in start date at Bethel from October 9th to the 16th. Approval was granted. That change in arrival date led to us meeting our new next door neighbors, Rick and Carol D, who would also arrive for their new assignment on October 16th. That would lead to a great friendship, as well as us knowing GB member Leo Greenlees better than we might have otherwise. Greenlees was on the elder body with Rick in the Greenpoint, Brooklyn congregation. Rick and Carol had been in that congregation already for years, Carol having grown up there.

Breaking Bread With the Governing Body

After finding out what building and room one is to now live in, and what congregation one has been assigned to, it's important to know where one is to eat each day. Work assignments and other things would be revealed later on.

Brooklyn Bethel had five dining rooms when we arrived. The Lower Dining room, which was in the basement of the 124 Columbia Heights building – the largest of the five, and where Russell and his cronies had historically eaten their meals and received instruction at Morning Worship – it was still used for that purpose until the properties were sold recently as of this writing. Of the other four, the one we were assigned to was the 4th Dining Room, in the semi-basement of the 124 building.

Each Bethel dining room table sat ten people - one at the head, one at the foot, and four on each side. Don Adams was our table "head," with his wife Dee sitting to his right. Only elders could be table heads. And only an appointed man could be a table foot, with his wife (if he was married) seated to his right. There was also a sort of seniority system to who sat closest to the head and foot. My wife and I sat smack in the middle, as we were lowest in rank.

What was different about our table, though, was that it was a Gilead table. A Gilead student, or two Gilead students who were married to each other, would sit nearest the foot, and at the foot sat a member of the GB, with his wife (if he was married) to his right. It was all part of the students getting to know each GB member in conjunction with their education that would send them out as missionaries to wherever in the world their assignment would be. The GB members rotated from table to table once each week on Monday, alphabetically according to their last names. Therefore, sitting at a Gilead table meant that all at the table would get to know the entire GB over the course of fifteen weeks, then the rotation would begin again, right back where it started. Breakfast and lunch, five days a week, every week.

I don't remember where in the alphabet our table started, but I do remember that Albert and Charlotte Schroeder were one of the early ones to meet and break bread with. The reason I remember that well is because it had to do with having previously met their son, Judah.

Judah (commonly called Judah Ben) is about my age, and worked in the Treasurer's Office (TO). I found out within two weeks of arriving at Bethel that I would be working in the Administrative Data part of the Computer Department, not the Publishing system as I had hoped. The first systems I would work on were for Cost Accounting (CA). CA does all of the accounting for the New York corporation (which oversees the US Branch), while TO handles accounting for the Pennsylvania corporation (which oversees all branches throughout the world). While my assignment initially involved working with CA overseer Harold Dies, staffer Joy Woody (sorry, women don't get titles at Bethel – but Joy is the person I worked most closely with and who knew their systems best – she was a very smart and funny woman, and as her name suggests, a joy to work with), and less with one of the three Rittenbach daughters who were all in Gilead school, I also frequently interacted with Judah. It was mainly casual conversation and horsing around though, because it would be a few years before I did any direct work with TO.

One day while eating lunch, I overheard Albert Schroeder talking about someone named Judah as if he were related to them, perhaps even being their son. My 22-year-old ears must have heard wrong. How can a GB member have a son? I turned to him and asked, "Excuse me, but are you talking about Judah Schroeder of the Treasurer's Office?"

"Yes."

"Oh, it sounds like you're related to him. Are you?"

"Yes. He's our son."

"Are you kidding?"

I had just that past summer had an uncomfortable experience with a prominent JW backstage at the District Convention at Belmont Racetrack. He was talking to me about crowd control and attendance counting, saying things that made no sense logistically. In fact they were ridiculous. I couldn't imagine that he would lie, or deliberately make me feel foolish by pulling my leg, so I sort of believed him. I asked, "Are you kidding me?"

The kidder replied, "No, that's how we do it."

I just looked at him incredulously and discontinued the conversation. Moments after he began his assembly part, the stage overseer, Monroe F (who was like a surrogate father to me), said, "Gary, he's pulling your leg," and then proceeded to delineate why what he was saying was absurd.

Well, I already knew it was absurd. Out of respect for an older man who was also a prominent one (I believe an ex-missionary who was then a District Overseer), I didn't call him out on it. Hence I was made to look and feel foolish. I hated that he did that.

One thing I learned from that right away, was how to not fall for something that has the ring of falsehood, regardless of who said it. The other thing that took much longer to learn is to not take myself and others too seriously, especially if respect for authority was on the line.

Back to Schroeder at the Gilead table.

I asked, "Are you kidding?"

He put down his fork, got very serious, and said, "Now why would I joke about a thing like that?"

I felt as if I had committed a great social faux-pas. I felt like a jerk.

I just said, "I don't know. I didn't think it was funny either. I just... I... I... I'm sorry."

No empathetic pat on the shoulder from Schroeder. No, "It's OK," followed by a casual anecdote about how a GB member can have a son at Bethel. Just a clear message of how to not be stupid in his presence.

The "publications" and other sources of direction from the GB have at times said things like, "Jehovah's people should not expect someone else to make decisions for them and give them a list of movies, books, and Internet sites to avoid." But at Bethel, it's different. Rules CAN be made about those things, because it is a "family," a group of people living in the same facility, working for the same "employer," and there must be certain family rules.

The release of a new Hollywood movie may especially generate considerable controversy within the Bethel family. Following the principle, "It is easier to get forgiveness than to get permission," some young Bethelites will deliberately go to a new movie at the earliest possible opportunity in order to see it before the GB can comment on it. Then they can always say, "You know, Brother Big-Opinion is right, Such-and-Such is not the kind of movie we should be watching. I know, because I made the mistake of seeing it before the counsel. I really regret it now." Nudge-nudge, wink-wink.

The 1982 release of Steven Spielberg's *E.T. The Extra Terrestrial* created such a stir.

Schroeder decided to take on the subject of extra-terrestrials one day when he was the chairman at Morning Worship. His treatise did not so much comment on the movie or the advisability of viewing it as it did the possibility of intelligent physical life other than on earth.

His logic went as follows:

If there is intelligent life in outer space, it would have to have been created by the same creator that made the human race. There is no other creator in the universe.

If he created another intelligent race, it would have to have been created with the same quality of free will as humans.

If the ETs have free will, they can use it wisely or foolishly, just like humans.

If they use it foolishly, they would have need for a redeemer, just like humans. Who could that redeemer be?

God's only-begotten son Jesus offered the one-time only, supreme sacrifice for humankind. He could not offer it again for another race. Any other heavenly being would be of lesser stature than Jesus, not in his unique position. That would not be fair or right for the ETs in question.

Therefore it is inconceivable that, at this time in history, there can be intelligent physical life anywhere in the universe other than earth. (Of course non-physical intelligent life can consist only of God, Jesus, angels, seraphs, and cherubs, as well as

Satan and the demons – entities we already know about.)

Add to that the fact that humankind is in the midst of a precedent-setting situation. After the issue of universal sovereignty is completely resolved, anyone that dares to raise the question again will be completely destroyed without risk to or effect on the rest of creation, according to Watchtower eschatology. So if God decides to populate other planets after that, he will do so any way he sees fit. But he can't do it yet. Not until the precedent has been set and resolved once for all time.

The overarching point is that there is no possibility that there is intelligent life anywhere in the universe beyond what we are already aware of. According to Schroeder.

Therefore, what is the point of seeing a movie about fantasies that contradict the Bible narrative? Who would come up with such an idea? In the words of Dana Carvey's Church Lady, "Could it be... SATAN?"

This logic was new to me. We had learned from our close association with Gilead students and the GB that there were many things taught in Gilead that are not in the publications, hence not known by other JWs. For example, all of the characters in the book of Job have prophetic significance. (I think Elihu is the Governing Body, Job's wife is the evil slave, and Job is, I dunno, Bugs Bunny or something. Of course I could be wrong.) Hence during Schroeder's discourse I thought for a moment that we were being treated to "special knowledge."

At some point my thoughts shifted to the possibility that Schroeder was losing his mind. Perhaps he was having a stroke. Whatever the case may be, something was wrong.

I kept those thoughts to myself, allowing the soup that Schroeder created to swirl around in my head over the following days and weeks.

My conclusion finally became that Schroeder is probably right. Even though his main points cannot be directly found in the Bible, they are based on principles involving sovereignty, free will, the ransom, and Watchtower eschatology and cosmology that MUST be right, since we have "the truth." Besides, how is it possible for a member of the GB, who had been the chief instructor at Gilead school for decades, to be wrong?

I have to admit that, even after being out for years as of this writing, I still wonder about his logic. I realize that to believe it because of the stature of the person who said it is to succumb to that logical fallacy called argumentum ad verecundiam. But I wonder about the logic itself.

However, the main character at the root of this example of argumentum ad verecundiam is not a man who was once a member of the GB. The main character is "the truth." For over forty years, "the truth" was, to me, the most powerful force in the universe. It allowed me to explain away vast abysses of utter nonsense in its name. It allowed me to excuse deplorable behavior on the part of some of its champions. It allowed me to live in the fog created by the notion that everything ever to be said by its source must and will also be truth, because it is "the truth."

Truth is truth, because it is truth.

That is perhaps the greatest of all logical fallacies.

I will leave it to the reader to unravel the E.T. logic any way one sees fit. My only recommendation is to NOT start from the position that if one has "the truth," the logic must be correct. Somehow I don't think anyone reading this will do that.

There was a closet just across the hall from our room on the third floor of the 107 building, a few doors down from the 107 library. One day, I got to wondering why our "garment" closet was on a different floor. Surely there had to be one available on our floor so that we could store various non-every-day personal items more accessibly. I had to see what was in that closet across the hall from us.

Among the various items existing in a state of disarray were a number of boxes bulging with documents. The only ones that caught my eye to the point where I read them in precise detail were correspondences between Schroeder and an "apostate" whose name I did not commit to memory. The two of them argued back and forth within letter after letter about various JW doctrines, the concept that God can have an "earthly" organization, and so forth. It seemed that Schroeder was faithfully upholding his loyalty to the organization, but at times his ideas also seemed unconventional.

I guess it's okay for a GB member to have such conversations because... well, because he's a GB member. If it were anyone else, a judicial committee would be convoked, and a lot of pain and misery dispensed.

Rank has its privileges.

Under the Rug

My ex-mother-in-law Wilma grew up in Norwich, a rural upstate New York town just under 200 miles NNW of New York City. Her Congregation Servant was a known pedophile. ("Congregation Servant" was roughly equivalent to today's Coordinator of the Body of Elders, but more The-Guy-Who-Ran-The-Whole-Show in those days.) He was often seen with his arm around certain young boys from the congregation openly, taking them to various places and in general acting inappropriately toward them publicly. According to Wilma, everyone in this small town knew what was going on. When word got back to Knorr about the scandal, he dispatched Arthur Worsley to investigate and fix it.

Wilma reminded me to look Worsley up when I got to Bethel. He was in the Correspondence Department, almost directly below my office, on the 4th floor of 25 Columbia Heights. I took a picture album with me that included a picture of him with sixteen-year-old Wilma and her sister Jean Harp. (In later years, Jean and her husband Ray Doosenberry served as Gilead missionaries in Spain.)

His face lit up immediately upon seeing that picture. He

explained that Knorr had sent him up to Norwich as a Circuit Overseer in the early 1950s because, "they had a congregation servant up there who was a Homo." ("Homo" was the word that the older men at Bethel typically used to refer to gay men, because "gay" dignifies them too much. Don Adams once corrected me when I used the less disparaging word, but I could never get used to their term, "homo.") The servant was replaced, but Worsley never told me what actually became of him.

Wilma's version of the story filled an important gap. Worsley had tapped her for what information she could provide without ever openly admitting to her or anybody else the nature of the problem. Among other things, she expressed her belief that God's spirit was with neither the congregation nor the organization, because of the pedophilia that she "and the whole town" knew of, as well as other scandals. He responded to her, "Yeah, we all think we know everything when we're sixteen."

Wilma subsequently ran away from home and the organization. She only returned about twenty years later, after she had moved to Hicksville, Long Island with her family that included the young girl that I would marry years later.

It's impermissible for an appointed man in the JW organization to ever admit any specific wrongdoing by another appointed man. If it means losing a gem like Wilma to "the world," so be it. Individuals don't matter. Only the reputation of the organization, the congregation, the elder body, (and supposedly Jehovah) matter.

Even as far back as the early- to mid-1950s, the JW organization's predilection for sweeping serious matters like pedophilia under the rug was alive and kicking.

It would be a few months after arriving at Bethel that we would have our ten meals per week every fifteen weeks with GB member Leo Greenlees. We would come to know him before that the same way any Bethelite does – passing in the hallways, or when it was his week as chairman at the head table in the Lower Dining Room, hence the chairman of Morning Worship. Additionally we had the mutual acquaintance of good friends Rick and Carol D, who were in his congregation, and Rick therefore on the same elder body with him.

The few single GB members typically exuded a special affection for the female family members. I don't mean an inappropriate one. I believe it was because women at Bethel typically don't have an agenda, therefore they are not out to impress anyone. They are refreshingly honest. After all, it's not as if they may put themselves in line for some sort of promotion within an organization that sees women as completely subservient to men. Compare that to many young male Bethelites that are clearly brown-nosing whenever in contact with a Bethel "heavy," and it's easy to see why a single GB member would feel a measure of comfort and relief in the presence of female family members.

Two single GB members that come to mind in that regard are John Booth and George Gangas. I mean it sincerely when I say it was a joy to see them light up when conversing with women.

I did not observe that tendency in Greenlees. His attention was drawn more to the young men than the young women.

I personally know very little about his past that I could write about definitively. One can easily look up his history with his longtime companion Percy Chapman if desired, but not having verification of the data it will neither be included nor commented on here.

Single male and female Bethelites with sufficient seniority can opt to room with someone of the same gender, or live by themselves in a "single," hence smaller, room. Greenlees preferred having a roommate. And he preferred, and always got, young roommates. All three of the other single GB members during my time at Bethel preferred to live alone, those being Booth, Gangas, and Fred Franz.

One day in early 1984 a surprise announcement was made by the chairman at Morning Worship that Leo Greenlees had been dismissed from the Governing Body and Bethel, and that the matter was closed. Had he been disfellowshipped for some reason, that fact would have been included in the announcement. It was not because he had not been.

Naturally Rick and I discussed the event. All Rick really told me beyond the nebulous was that Greenless had explained that the GB had dismissed him for something he did, and that, "They were right" to do so. He had also assured his young roommate of that.

The obligation of everyone was to carry on as usual without discussing the matter. That is what we all did.

In the months and years ahead, the silence about Greenlees was deafening. After that table announcement, his name never came up again in any program, or any publication of the Society with one nebulous exception related to a part he had done on a Gilead Graduation program while he was still a GB member. He died about four years later, on February 17th, 1988, while still "in good standing" with the organization. Silence.

In early 1984 the father of a grade school-aged boy from the

Bronx, (I will use the boy's initials, "MP"), took a trip to Brooklyn to lodge a complaint about Greenlees.

The father and mother had been doing Finnish translation work for Watchtower. MP has testified as an adult that, during one of their trips to Bethel in the 1970s, "a Bethel family member sexually molested me, or raped me. His name was Leo Greenlees, and I was not his only victim." When the father learned of this in 1984, he was furious and brought the accusation right to headquarters without an appointment. Somehow he gained an audience and presented the case, threatening that he would go to the authorities if Greenlees was not removed from his position.

Soon thereafter Leo Greenlees was dismissed from the Governing Body and Bethel.

At the time I was not aware of those circumstances involving the young boy. I'm not sure who might have known about them, besides the man, his son, and the men that handled the case.

Conversations with people who should know, namely other GB members, have been telling. I have talked with a number of GB members (see chapter entitled Hairy Carey) about the most famous "apostate" of our modern age, Raymond Franz. At that time and for years after (and I assume right up until today), they had no problem stating very clearly that he was an apostate, even describing some conversations as well as deliberations with Ray at GB meetings from their point of view only. They would vilify and tear him apart at every opportunity. Conversely, when talking to those same men about Greenlees, they simply have said things like, "that's not something we can discuss," or, "the matter is closed."

Does that constitute a smoking gun? If a man really didn't do a whole lot wrong, why can it not be discussed at least in general to some small degree?

If Greenlees were innocent of the charges, but guilty of something far less damning, it would not be inappropriate to say something like, "He committed a minor indiscretion that called his qualifications into question. A member of the Governing Body has to be irreprehensible to a greater degree than others." That would be understandable, wouldn't it? It might even tend to lay the matter to rest.

If an appointed man who is in the know cannot make such a simple statement, it is because the simple, relatively innocent statement is not true. There is something more serious involved.

Saint George the Owl

Our first room at Bethel was on the third floor of the 107 Columbia Heights building. Two doors down from us was the Gilead library. The office of GB member George Gangas was at the far end of that library, and he lived on the other end of that same floor in a single-man room. He had to walk past our room and through the library every time he went back and forth.

We usually called him Brother Gangas to his face, but for reasons that should become obvious in a moment, also at times referred to him as George. I will usually refer to him as George in this text, as I associate that with some fond memories.

For every time I interacted with George, my wife probably did so ten times. It got to the point where he wouldn't trek between his room and office without stopping to say Hello if one or both of us were there, and often have a significant conversation. Usually with my wife. He was one of the single men I was referring to when I said they mostly enjoyed the company of young women when the setting was casual. He and my wife became good friends.

We had a ceramic owl in our room that stood about the height of my knees positioned on the floor right next to our door. During one of George's visits, he asked if the owl had a name. My wife responded in the negative. George then said, "We'll name him after me. Saint George!"

That owl continued to be called Saint George for decades after we moved back to Long Island, and then to Sussex County in New Jersey. We loved telling that story.

And we loved George, the man the owl was named after.

George was an affable man. Sort of cute. Comical, in an unintentional way. I don't even remember what his job was on the GB, or what committees he served on. I think his job in that library office had something to do with personnel. It didn't matter. He was a GB member, hence we thought every second of every one of his days was full of ultra-important activity. What did we know?

Everyone who has ever met George knows at least two things about him. First, he was a voracious student of the Bible. His love for it was unmistakable and obvious. That leads to the second, even more noticeable thing.

George loved plying people with Bible questions. Even if he

just came across you in the hallway, he more than likely would stop you in your tracks to at least ask you to name the twelve apostles, or the twelves tribes of Israel.

Some people dreaded his questions, hence they avoided him, because they didn't like being put on the spot. I, on the other hand, waited patiently yet anxiously for my turn. I don't know why in the world it took so long, since I saw him all the time. But one day, while we were eating breakfast, he asked me to name the eleven covenants in the Bible. At least I think the number was eleven. I dunno, I'm in my early sixties as of this writing. What do I know about numbers, or anything?

Right away I named a couple of them, starting with the rainbow covenant after the Noachian flood. He said, "That is not a covenant."

"It's not a covenant? It's always referred to as 'the rainbow covenant,' isn't it?"

"Who is it between?"

"It's between God and... well, it's not between God and Noah... It's between God and all mankind."

"But God was only speaking to Noah. He did not refer to anyone else."

"Okay, then it was between God and... Noah?"

"What did Noah have to do that to uphold his side of the covenant?"

"Um. I don't know. I don't think it says anything about Noah doing anything. He had already done a lot."

"A covenant is between two entities. When one entity does what he said he would do, the other entity is obligated to do what he said he would do. What was Noah's obligation?"

After a pregnant pause, I simply said, "I'll have to research that."

That morning at work I pulled *Aid To Bible Understanding* off my bookshelf and opened to the article on Covenants. As I suspected, the rainbow covenant was discussed in the article. I studied the facts about it, also noting all the other covenants, and brought my results to George the same day at lunch.

"The *Aid* book says it's a covenant."

"Does it? How does it say that?"

"It doesn't say, the rainbow covenant 'is a covenant,' but it's in the article on covenants, as part of a list."

"Because it's in an article on covenants that makes it a covenant?"

"Well, no. But it's referred to as, 'the rainbow COVENANT.'"

"How does it meet the definition of a covenant?"

Another pregnant pause later, and I said, "All right, it's not a covenant. But why does the *Aid* book appear to list it as one?"

George proceeded to give me a brief lesson on looking beyond the obvious, using the power of reason, and finding the real meat.

George was an early riser. Every day, without exception, he would be up by around 5:00 AM. He would use all of that time before 7:00 AM Morning Worship and then breakfast to study the Bible. One day, when my photographer friend and fellow musician Mike L was working on a project that involved getting individual pictures of many Bethel family members, he stopped by George's room. George was in his bathrobe, but didn't object to having his picture taken. It just had to be a picture of him reading the Bible. He also thought he should be dressed better. So he put on a short sleeve dress shirt. Over his robe. Mike now had a picture of GB member George Gangas reading the Bible in his bathrobe, with a short sleeve shirt over it. You can't make this stuff up.

GB members are not great congregation meeting attenders. They blame it on their multitudinous and profoundly important responsibilities. George, on the other hand, was seldom missing from the Murray Hill congregation meetings on the Upper East Side of New York's Manhattan Borough. Also, we were in the same circuit. I don't recall him ever missing a Circuit Assembly. Not because he had weighty assembly parts. In fact, the only time I recall seeing him on stage was when he was interviewed as part of a panel of four or so people, talking about Bible studies and preaching in general.

With him on that panel was a young woman he had found in the door to door work, studied with, and brought to baptism. I believe she was around thirty years old. She told her version of their story, after which George had his turn. At the end of George's brief interview, from his seat, he waved his large-print Bible over his head, and with a raised voice, told the audience to, "Talk, talk, talk, talk, talk!!"

We might not agree with JW's teachings, or the advisability of being a member of that organization. The point is that George was honestly doing what he understood to be the most important thing in the world to do.

He was the real deal.

On any given weekend day, if one walked around Brooklyn Heights, especially to one of the subway stations at Clark Street or Cadman Plaza, one might have seen George doing street work. His zeal was true and heartfelt. The only other GB member I have ever observed doing that work was Martin Pötzinger, with his wife Gertrude.

George is a big part of the reason why I believe that not all GB members see the organization as a cult. Some of them were just as fooled as the rest of us. Of course that's just my opinion that the reader is free to disagree with. But consider this. They weren't always GB members – they were all once children, many of them raised as JWs, probably by sincere parents who wanted the best for them. They then became pioneers, ministerial servants, elders, and so on, all the while believing they had "the truth," and making excuses for organizational lapses, just as we may have. By the time they have been groomed to be on the GB and settled into their positions, they have long experienced what it's like to be elders who see a lot of nonsense but can excuse it away on the basis of the JWs still being "the only organization on earth that God is using." I am not making excuses for them. I am just being honest and realistic. I also believe that, conversely, there may have been some, and likely are now, who know the truth about the organization's cult status. It's just not for me to list them on the basis of which side of good vs evil they may be on. I'm just offering my personal experiences – the rest is up to the reader.

Just a few more brief stories about George that I can't help but include here.

One day my wife lost her Bethel ID. A Bethel ID looked like a driver's license, and was necessary to get into any of the Bethel buildings. Even if one is George Gangas, one is supposed to show ID upon entry – a conscientious attendant will not allow entry without it.

She was in a quandary as to what to do about the loss of her ID. I suggested we just report it to Bethel Office, and take it from there. Then we ran into George in the tunnel between the 124 and 107 buildings. She asked him what she should do. He said, "Forget about it. Someone will find it and turn it in."

She thought that was the greatest idea ever. After going on our way, I quietly told her what a bad idea that was, and that we should just tell Bethel Office.

But George was the GB member. I was just her little old insignificant husband. She did it George's way. At first. When her ID never turned up, she finally went to Bethel Office. They gave her a new ID. Nothing short of a miracle, but not a victory for me.

One time after the Monday night Family Watchtower study in the 107 Kingdom Hall, we were all exiting the Kingdom Hall to go home. Carol D for some reason was wearing a hand puppet on her right hand. We walked right beside George in the crowd. When he looked up at Carol, (yes, up – he was a short, hunched over man), and smiled as only he does, and asked what she had there, she quickly grabbed his nose with the puppet and said, "Gotcha!" He laughed and enjoyed that moment immensely. I cringed. If a young man like me did that to a GB member... But it was a young woman, so George was more than OK with it. And I became OK with it after witnessing his response.

There were certain things that George was famous for saying. Over and over and over.

When giving a talk having anything to do with sexual morality, he would time and again say, "How could someone give up EVERLASTING LIFE for a few MOMENTS of sensual pleasure?"

I don't know how many times I heard those same exact words, until one day they were forever changed to, "How could someone give up EVERLASTING LIFE for a few HOURS of sensual pleasure?"

I guess he must have finally been privy to some real-life cases of hanky-panky. Sometimes it was hard to suppress a laugh when he was talking.

My last George story has to do with his public prayers.

Every single one of his prayers would at some point include telling the one he was praying to how we're looking forward to the day when all mankind will see that he is a, "true, and loving, kind, forgiving, wonderful, compassionate God," and I dunno, probably another dozen or so adjectives. "And that Satan is a gross, wicked, monstrous, debased, terrible, and evil liar," and just as many adjectives for the second guy as the first guy, except they were worse adjectives.

Gangas was kooky, but real.

I miss my owl.

SEX

I had always imagined that listening to the various luminaries at Bethel speak on a daily basis would be like the last talk of the District Convention on steroids. Stories about the work in other countries, progress in the worldwide ministry, maybe some inside dope on when the end is actually coming. Ya know, super-cool, ethereal stuff.

Within the first month of our assimilation into our new home, rather than hearing generous morsels of heavenly wisdom descending on a golden beam of light, we heard announcements of various Bethelites who had been disfellowshipped. At least once a week, or more often, like two or three times a week. It was getting to be like a plague. I began to think it was normal, like it happens all the time. Then I did a little math and wondered how the family could still consist of about 3,600 people with a dozen or so new arrivals every week, and so many MORE leaving one way or the other.

Then one morning it was announced that no overnight guests would be allowed at the Monday night Watchtower study. Customarily, every other Monday night included a special talk after the study that fulfilled my desire to peer into the spiritual stratosphere for an additional hour. The "no overnight guests" decree seemed too ominous to allow for that eventuality. Seasoned Bethelites knew exactly what was to transpire. I just waited, wondered and worried.

The program had to do with the reason for all the disfellowshipping. It was all about sex.

The chairman and all of the presenters were GB members. They wanted to send a crystal clear message that this was serious business. The reason why no overnight guests were permitted to be in attendance was that they didn't want them hearing how screwy things can be at the world headquarters, right under the noses of the men with the direct line to the heavenly throne.

I don't recall them talking about sexual immorality between men and women. Maybe they did. I just remember what came next. To appreciate the gravity of it, one must first take into the account the moral precepts of Watchtower when it comes to sexual morality. What follows is a little trip down Memory Lane for all post-JW readers. According to Watchtower's interpretation of the Greek word πορνεία (porneia), fornication is sex between or among any persons who are not legally and scripturally married to each other. (Gay people who ARE legally married to each other don't get a free pass – their marriages are not considered scriptural, so even sex with their mates would be fornication, but especially yucky fornication.) But wait, there's more. Even though the penalty for unrepentant fornication, no matter who it is between, is ultimately eternal destruction, there is a special repugnance for homosexual sex. Perhaps because the divinely constituted punishment for gays is identical to that of heterosexual offenders, there is a need to single out gays for special vilification prior to Armageddon. Judge 'em before God can.

If the JWs ever tumble to the fact that the stated punishment for all unforgiven sin is the same, and come to grips with the gravity of blatant religious hypocrisy, they will realize that there are going to be a lot of heterosexuals in the same theoretical eternal dumpster as the gays. And it is doubtful that any pedophile, regardless of theocratic rank, will have any special privileges there.

The fact is, homosexuality had become quite popular among Bethel family members. Most of the recently disfellowshipped were of that persuasion. The GB speakers at this special event would have us believe that it all usually starts with solo masturbation. Unfortunately for them, that practice had been excluded from the definition of fornication, hence removed from the list of disfellowshipping offenses, quite a number of years prior to 1980. They could now only describe it as "unclean." But, since it is a "stepping stone" to homosexuality, it's damn serious. Excessive slapping of the salami may even be considered "loose conduct." I guess loose conduct is somewhere between uncleanness and disfellowshipping worthy. Even when I was an elder, I could never get that subtle distinction straight in my mind. Probably since it really doesn't matter.

A number of young men (it's always the young ones causing problems!) had been practicing masturbation. (In reality, most people do, JWs included.) Even more egregious, some roommates were engaging in playful wrestling – in their underwear. Inappropriate touching occurs, and the next thing you know, we have a new homosexual convert.

So stop doing that, boys.

The homosexual club got so extensive that groups of young Brooklyn Bethelite men would make two-hour weekend trips to Watchtower Farms (or vice versa) and have sex with their friends, in a kind of exchange program. The question, "Do you want to come over for a rum and Coke?" became code for, "Do you want to fuck?"

What was discussed next may even have shocked any pedophiles in the ranks.

An unstated number of Watchtower Farms Bethelites,

apparently all men (at least one married), had been practicing bestiality. The only specific cases we learned about were of men having calves perform oral sex on them. Who knows what else may have been happening at the farm where cattle, pigs, and chickens were in abundance.

A secondary consequence of this situation was that all animals that were identified as having sex with any humans were destroyed, and not used for food or any other purpose. How that identification was performed with any accuracy is anyone's guess. Did they rely on information provided by the sexual deviants? I have always wondered whether there was some kind of Biblical principle involved with that decision, if it was based on the science of hygiene, or both.

Naturally this information was discussed ad infinitum by the family at work, the dining room tables, while traveling to congregation meetings, and so on. I recall some saying that they remembered hearing Nathan Knorr talk turkey like that to the family all of the time, and they actually missed those good old days.

It also became fodder for much humor. One of the most memorable jokes was that there would now be a requirement to leave the barn door open when alone with the animals. To understand that joke requires an understanding of one of the tenets in *Dwelling Together in Unity*, the manual that was issued to all Bethelites and that delineated certain codes of conduct for them. In it is a prohibition on a male and female who are non-married, a non-nuclear family of ever being alone in a room together. If it happens due to reasonable circumstances, they should keep the door wide open. That should explain the barn joke. (Sorry, I just broke the rule that says if you have to explain a joke, it wasn't funny. You have permission to reread the joke and its explanation in reverse order and laugh anyway, if you're so inclined.)

What the logic of the prohibition doesn't explain is how it is still permissible for many hundreds of males to room with other males, obviously with their doors only open as long as it takes to walk through the doorway. Especially as it is widely recognized that a certain percentage of the world population is innately gay. Of course Watchtower doesn't recognize that innateness, therefore all homosexual behavior is viewed as unnatural and controllable. Either way, how is it that two males may get away with innocent behavior that a male and a female may not? Watchtower's strict moral code creates certain contradictions.

Another thing I always found fascinating is connected with other unrelated occasions when a man would be disfellowshipped for having sex with a women he is not married to, whether inside or outside the Bethel family. Invariably they would search his room and find a treasure trove of pornography. That fact would be announced to the family in terms of the weight of the stash, as in, "In one man's room five pounds of pornographic material was found." (Interestingly, in at least once case, Victoria's Secret catalogs were included in the definition of "pornography.") They had to weigh it? The degree of sin is directly proportional to the weight of the porn magazines? It would be nice to have time to waste on such pointless nonsense.

The Umpire

The first time I met Dan Sydlik in person was not long after our arrival at Bethel, in one of the dining rooms. After lunch, my wife and I greeted him and told him how he was instrumental in us being accepted by and invited to headquarters, and thanked him for his help. He replied, "Well, when you start having problems, forget about me."

Dan was the favorite of nearly every young man who ever served at Bethel simultaneously to him. Based on that reputation I tended to like him at first also. He spoke their language. He was down to earth, and wasn't afraid to get on their level with them. For example, in the summers, when the young men would use their lunch break to play softball in a small park between the factory and home, Dan would umpire the games. Missing lunch at one's regular table was considered a selfish act of disloyalty to many old-school Bethelites, since the waiters would shut down tables that were sparsely populated and the remaining people would have to find an empty seat at another table (or two seats for married couples). It was called "supporting your table." (Missing breakfast was worse than missing the annual Memorial celebration, due to its strong spiritual component. It was a sign that there may be something wrong.) But Dan would of course miss lunch, along with all of the other scoff-laws that opted for the softball game. His young wife Marina would hold down the fort at the Gilead table on those days.

In his T-shirt, he would carry out his umpiring duties in an animated fashion. And the players would interact with him like they would any other umpire.

He would yell, "Yer OUT!"

"What?? I was safe by a mile!"

"You were OUT by a mile, son!"

"Are you BLIND? I got to the base a week before the ball did!"

"Yer OUT cuz I SAID yer out!"

Of course Dan the Man was right because he was the umpire, and not because he was a GB member.

His sense of humor enabled him to be a bit of a prankster at times. Like the time he had just boarded an elevator in the Towers building. He was standing at about the middle of the car, facing out, when a young man tried to enter. Without a word, Dan lifted his folded umbrella horizontal to the floor, placed the finial at the top in the young man's breadbox, and pushed him out of the elevator with it.

That was typical of the kind of games he would play, mostly with the young men.

One Sunday night, when I was on line in the Lower Dining Room to get supper to bring back to our room, Dan pulled up behind me. Sunday meals, breakfast and supper only, were cafeteria style. They consisted of simple things like the macaroni and cheese I was fetching for us and our room full of guests. I proceeded to fill a huge Tupperware bowl with mac & cheese, to the point of embarrassment. I had to let Dan know that I was feeding an entire room full of people without appearing self-righteous about it by apologizing for nothing.

I glanced at him out of the corner of my eye and said, "My wife is REALLY hungry."

Dan replied with his deep, resonant voice, "She must be a COW!"

Thinking quickly, I countered, "No, but she is Italian."

I may be the only person ever to leave Dan speechless. We both had a good laugh.

Dan was the GB's representative on the Family Night Committee. There were certain members of the Bethel Family, including at least one GB member (Ted Jaracz), that didn't agree with the concept of Family Night. Dan was there to smooth things over and allow everyone to relax and enjoy themselves in spite of the minority of anal retentive judges.

Family Night was a variety show put on by members of the family for the family. We would have three per year, taking a break for summer conventions and vacations. It featured musical performances, skits, interviews, and even dancing on at least one occasion. Rehearsals would transpire for the months leading up to the first performance for the family, which was always on a Wednesday night. The "real" performances were the following Saturday and Sunday nights.

During our time at Bethel, the Family Night Committee consisted of Merton Campbell, Michael Saint Jean, Ciro Aulicino, Stanley Snail, and Dan Sydlik. The chairmanship would rotate among them each new show, excluding Dan. He would come for the last rehearsal and dress rehearsal before the Wednesday night performance. He would approve or disapprove of parts, offer suggestions, and so on. The regular committee members had likely already rid the show of parts that would offend the more persnickety members of the family, so there usually wasn't much that Dan found objectionable. In fact, more often than not, his comments were concerned with spicing things up a bit.

For our first Family Night my wife and I were both just audience members. Being a performing musician, I was bitten by the bug that night and yearned to participate. After that season's show, while preparations were beginning for the next one, I learned that no one who is currently in Bethel Entrants School was permitted to participate. Being that we were at the beginning of our first year, we would be in Entrants School for some months to come. However, a man in my department, Roger T, knew of my piano playing, and asked me to join him, Beatrice B, and Fred F, in an eight-handed version of Franz Liszt's *2nd Hungarian Rhapsody*, (two pianos and four pianists). Somehow, an exception was made and I was allowed to participate. I was on every Family Night after that as a pianist for all our time at Bethel.

As the rehearsals progressed, I saw the opportunity to have my opposed, non-JW parents attend the show. I thought it would be a wonderful way to show them that Bethel consists of real people who do real things, including having some fun once in a while. Being that my family was originally from Brooklyn, I had them visit at times, not only touring the facilities and spending time in our room, but also walking around beautiful Brooklyn Heights. That neighborhood was in much better shape and more gentrified than any other part of Brooklyn or Queens they had ever lived in. Showing them what was going on in the Publishing side of the Computer Department demonstrated the unusual degree of technical expertise being utilized there, and meeting some of the department's personnel exposed them to some of the most intensely intelligent people I or they had ever known. Family Night would be the icing on the cake. I thought they might actually be proud of me. Or something like that.

However, only Bethelites and overnight guests were allowed to attend Family Night. Folks who lived as close as my family did, about thirty miles east of Brooklyn Heights, would not qualify as overnight guests. Additionally, it was exceedingly rare for non-JWs to be overnight guests. (I only know of one instance, when Shelby S died in a car accident, and his mostly non-JW family, including military personnel, were treated royally as overnight guests.) Someone suggested I speak to Dan about having an exception made.

I called him on the phone and explained the circumstances, but without mentioning that my parents were not JWs.

"Hi, Brother Sydlik. This is Gary Alt. I'm one of the four

people who are playing the Liszt piece on two pianos at the upcoming Family Night. How are you doing?"

"Fine. What can I do for you?"

"Well, my parents would like to attend one of the performances. I understand that they would have to be overnight guests, but they can't be because they live too close to Brooklyn."

"Where do they live?

"Westbury. In central Nassau County, just past the Queens border. I guess it's about thirty miles from here. I was wondering if you might be able to help."

"There is a possibility, but I can't say just yet. Call me back as we get closer to the show."

"Okay, like in a few weeks?"

"Yes, that would be fine."

"Thanks, Brother Sydlik. Oh, can I ask you one more thing?"

"Go ahead."

"If they can come, will they be able to sit in Towers Assembly Hall, where the performance is, instead of one of the dining rooms?"

Dan evidently thought that was a very brash and impudent thing to say. He heightened his volume and pitch dramatically, as he said, "What do you want, front row seats??"

Oops. I had pushed too far. The only thing I could think to do was make light of my gaffe with a little humor. Through a slight titter, I sheepishly said, "Yeah, maybe they could sit on the stage with me."

Dan raised his voice further with clear indignation and barked, "Don't get wise with me, boy, or they won't come at all!!"

My heart sank. All I managed to say was something stupid, like, "Yes sir, of course. I'll call you in a few weeks. Bye."

I never called him about that matter again. I just assumed my parents would not be able to attend. The trick was how to explain it to them, since I had already built them up about it. I don't remember what I told them, but the worst thing about it was that my opportunity to show my opposed parents something good and positive about my new life was now closed.

Despite those negative developments, that Family Night was some of the most fun I have ever had. What made it especially exciting was that GB member Karl Klein and his wife Margareta were the interviewees on that show. Karl was a great lover of music, and gushed with enthusiasm whenever we talked about our performance of the Liszt *Hungarian Rhapsody*. More about that in a later chapter.

On another Family Night, a few years later, I played with a jazz band assembled by a young bass player. It included me on piano, a drummer, the bass player (I have forgotten both of their names), and Ricky Hanagami on trumpet. (Sometime later I played at a wedding in Philadelphia with what I think was essentially the same band, but included Jay Buckey on guitar.) Ricky was the overseer of the shoe department, and an exceedingly meek young man who was also skilled in karate. A one page story of an encounter between him and a would-be thief is in the 9/22/86 *Awake!*, page 16. Just don't let me catch anyone reading those magazines!

We used to rehearse on the stage in the Towers Assembly Hall. We noticed that at nearly every rehearsal, a lone man would be sitting in the same spot in the audience. No one recognized him. We finally asked him if he liked what he was hearing, and a conversation ensued.

He was visiting from the Netherlands branch. He was in Brooklyn learning how to reassemble the Mann printing press that was being replaced by a new, much bigger press, taken apart, and shipped to the Netherlands. He was also a saxophone player, who played regularly with a jazz band of some 20 to 30 players at his branch. We asked him to join us for a jam. He enthusiastically said yes and returned with his sax to play.

All of our songs were traditional pieces from the 1930-50s, like *I Only Have Eyes For You, On the Sunny Side of the Street,* and *Red Roses For a Blue Lady.* I wish I could remember his name, but since I can't we're stuck with calling our then-new friend from Holland, "the sax player."

The sax player blended in with us instantaneously, and our songs began to morph into more of the Dixieland genre. He and Ricky would weave in and out of each other, turning those old pop songs into New Orleans style jazz.

The next, obvious questions were, "How long will you be in Brooklyn?" and, "Would you like to play with us on Family Night?"

He would be in Brooklyn just beyond Family Night, and, yes,

he wanted to play with us.

That night I made a beeline to current FN Committee chairman Mike Saint Jean's room to present the idea to him and get a buy-in. Mike was a relatively young man, perhaps in his late thirties or early forties, who worked in the Service Department. He had a suave, sophisticated appearance that set him apart from the rest of the Bethelites. His blonde hair was combed in a way that was contrary to common Bethel etiquette, and he typically wore smooth looking flare pants with sleek leather shoes. It was well after 9:00 PM when I got to Mike's room in the Towers building, not a time one would normally be knocking on the door of someone who, like all of us, had to rise around 6:00 AM to be ready for Morning Worship and breakfast at 7:00 AM, then make it to work by 8:00 AM. But he was happy to see me.

Mike listened attentively, and slowly but surely his face lit up as he thought about the idea.

I asked him, "So what do you think?"

"Yeah, yeah, that sounds like a great idea. Yeah, I think we should do it. Of course I have to run it by the other committee members. But I think it'll be great."

"Cool. Thanks Mike! Have a good night!"

Getting a jazz band WITH A DRUM SET past the committee had already been a mammoth task. Now, with Mike's help, we were going to try to slip in a horn player who was NOT a Brooklyn Bethelite.

Our idea was subsequently approved.

At the final rehearsal before our first performance, Dan made his appearance. I crossed my pagan fingers as I waited for his response to our playing.

He didn't say much at first. Not until someone suggested that perhaps the sax player could switch to clarinet, as it was less strident and "noisy."

Dan finally chimed in, "I wanna hear more horn! Gimme more horn! I wanna hear that horn!"

Then he made a suggestion that I thought was crazy.

"I want the audience to really hear this horn. I want him to walk around the audience during his solo on the last song. Tell 'em like it used-to-was!"

Okay, so let's get this straight. We were going to be the first Family Night act to feature drums. Now we had a trumpet and sax wailing like Louis Armstrong and Charlie Parker. And the sax player is gonna leave the stage and blow that thing practically in the laps of a Bethel audience? Isn't that being a bit too showboat, getting the audience worked up, and focusing attention on the creation, rather than the creator?

Well, who was going to argue with Dan? We tried his idea. Everybody loved it. When we did it in the three performances for the family, the audiences also loved it. To hell with Jaracz, Dean Songer, and all the other Puritans – they don't come to Family Night anyway!

Musician friend Mike L, (remember the fellow with the camera in George's room?), said to me, "You've set a new standard for Family Night."

That was perhaps one of my favorite musical moments of my life. And I've had many great ones.

On another Family Night I played piano for the whole show except for one song. We were doing a "Room Bid" skit. (Look up "Room Bid" in the index for a brief explanation of what that is.) There was a scene that was supposed to be Abraham in the new system, or something like that. An outdoor, bright and peaceful morning kind of a scene. They wanted a flute to play some appropriate background music. I borrowed a flute from my friend Bruce G and played *Morning Mood* from Edvard Grieg's *Peer Gynt Suite No. 1.*

During the final rehearsal, Dan shouted out, "I want to hear more Grieg!"

I sheepishly replied across the room, "You'll have to find someone who actually knows how to play the flute."

I knew of Bruce G well before we ever met at Bethel. He was in the Glen Cove, Long Island congregation, where two of our Westbury elders had been for years. They used to speak of his considerable intelligence often. He became a Bethelite about halfway through our time there. Bruce played French horn, and he assembled a trio that consisted of himself on horn, me on piano, and a violinist from Long Island whose first name is Greg. We played the final movement of Brahms' *Trio for Piano, Horn and Violin in E-flat major.* (I recall later walking up to Ciro's office in the Writing Department to lend him my copy of the album that featured that piece. Ciro had a great love for classical music that led to many wonderful conversations between us.)

Bruce was assigned to a congregation in Bedford Stuyvesant, where he served on the elder body with Dan Sydlik. It was a very small elder body, just three or four men. Meanwhile, back in Glen Cove, Bruce's mother was not doing well. Being that he was the only one in the family in a position and willing to help her, he was dividing his time more and more among Bethel, Bed Stuy, and Glen Cove.

One day Bruce approached my wife and me about joining him as the first Bethelites to serve Glen Cove. It was the only way he could manage to stay at Bethel and take care of his mother. The Service Department would never approve of him going by himself, and it would likely not be economically feasible anyway. So he needed us, or someone else willing to help. Realizing it would be a heck of a drive, especially for mid-week meetings, we agreed and said we would love to do it.

There was only one problem. Dan Sydlik. Dan told Bruce he was needed in Bed Stuy, especially as Dan could not always be there. When Bruce explained his situation and persisted, Dan said he would, "block it," if it went to the Service Department for approval.

Bruce informed us that the idea would not work. My response

was, "If you have to leave Bethel and return to Glen Cove to care for you mother, Sydlik and Bed Stuy are gonna lose you anyway. Doesn't Dan know that? What's he gonna do if you don't follow his wishes, if you apply to Service anyway? What's the worst that can happen? They say "No?" So what? Bruce, you'll never know unless you try."

"There's no way it's going to work. Dan has too much power and influence. It won't work."

"Maybe it won't. Or maybe it will. One thing is for sure, if you don't even try, it CERTAINLY won't work. If you do try, maybe it'll turn out for the best."

In the end, Bruce succumbed to Dan's pressure, did not apply for the transfer, and eventually had to leave Bethel anyway.

Each year while we were at Bethel, we would go to the Bethel meetings at the District Conventions, just to support the event and answer any questions.

One year Dan was conducting the Bethel meeting in the Chairman's office of the Nassau Coliseum.

When speaking about the kinds of workers Bethel was looking for, he advised everyone attending to think about a vocation that requires at least a two-year college degree, and to obtain that degree. Bethel does not just need press room workers, bindery workers, housekeepers and so on. They need skilled, certified plumbers, electricians, engineers, and so on.

Square that with the general belief that higher education was banned by Watchtower. It wasn't, at least not in those days. In some cases it was even recommended.

So the GB wasn't responsible for a general attitude throughout much of the organization that college is verboten. It was the misinterpretation and tendency to make draconian rules on the part of local elders, family heads, and others. Right?

The fact is, it is the Governing Body that promotes obedience to local elders, regardless of the degree they might be straying from official doctrine. Because to do otherwise would detract from the aura of Holy Spirit in the appointment process. Therefore, who is to blame if many of us have had skewed ideas of what is required vs what is forbidden as officially stated by the GB? Is it not the GB itself that allows false information to take root and grow, without batting an eye?

Could It Be... Satan?

In early 1982, rumors created by the Trinity Broadcasting Network stated that certain rock stars were cooperating with the Church of Satan to place hidden subliminal messages in music records. That same year, fundamentalist Christian pastor Gary Greenwald held public lectures on the insidious influence of backmasking, along with at least one mass record-smashing event. Before the year was out, thirty North Carolina teenagers, led by their pastor, claimed that singers had been possessed by Satan, who used their voices to create backward messages. They then held a record-burning at their church.

The backmasking scare was clearly fundamentalist in origin. It took over the brainwaves of many Bethelites, and indeed many throughout the JW organization. (Backmasking is not to be confused with backward masking, which is a legitimate recording technique.)

Music came under attack at Bethel. It was amazing to me to see how many people believed the hype just because it was all pinned on Satan. Watchtower had clearly adopted a stance that originated in, wait for it... Christendom!

However, Watchtower took it a step further, employing the idea that the entire world is under Satan's control. Especially is the entertainment industry under his control. Of all of the sub-genres of that industry, music is apparently the most nefarious. Therefore it's not a stretch to believe that Satan would use the industry he already owns and controls, to infect our minds with the use of backward messages. I don't believe there was ever any conclusion on just how that worked. Did the evil one influence the songwriters to write words that would say something different backward? Or did he use them as puppets to sing with just the right phrasing and inflections to do the trick? Or did he use his pernicious powers to alter the electronic and other devices to produce the coded messages? There was never any conclusion on those questions because NONE OF IT MADE A DAMN BIT OF SENSE.

Talk about Satan and his henchmen became ubiquitous throughout all Bethel activities: at work, at meals, on public transportation, and even at the family Watchtower study.

Reports of obedient, conscientious young Bethelites disposing of some or all of their record collections in hoppers and dumpsters were regularly read to the family. During one such report, Home Overseer George Couch held up an album cover to the camera and said, "Just look at this cover. Do we have to wonder about the demonic content of the music? Isn't it obvious from the cover?"

The album was King Crimson's *In the Court of the Crimson King*. Admittedly, the artwork is on the grotesque side. It apparently depicts the *21st Century Schizoid Man,* one of the songs on the album. The lyrics to that song have absolutely nothing to do with demonism or the occult. The song is a sort of protest against war and the political state of the world. The genre of King Crimson's music is best described as progressive rock. It combines elements of classical and jazz. The personnel of the band has been a revolving door, and features some of the most talented and respected musicians of our age. It is not "hard" rock, "acid" rock, or any other moniker one may wish to conjure up in order to vilify the band and its music.

Couch seriously missed the boat on that one. It was a textbook case of gross ignorance, judging the contents of something with zero knowledge about it. The expression, "You can't judge a book by its cover" comes to mind.

Another album cover that drew considerable attention was the one that is commonly referred to as *Santana III*. The artwork is reminiscent of imagery associated with the film *2001: A Space Odyssey,* although there is no connection. The music combines blues and rock with Latin percussion and jazz fusion. (Carlos Santana is from Mexico and started his career in San Francisco, California, after his father moved the family there for his work.) As with the music of King Crimson, there is no connection to demonism or the occult.

My reaction to all the record dumping was to scour the various bins for anything I might be interested in that wasn't already in my collection. Being a very big fan of Carlos Santana, I was subsequently able to complete that segment of my collection. I'm more than happy to capitalize on others' lack of vision, as long as no one gets hurt.

In the early 1980s, when a Bethelite was to be a panelist at the family Watchtower study, (a member of an ad hoc "congregation" within the assembly), he would receive a note in his room from Bethel Office stating the date of the study, and the part of the paragraph he was to comment on. Only elders and ministerial servants qualified for this privilege, so of course they were all men. There would be several weeks to prepare the answer that would make or break a man's reputation within the family, as to whether he was a self-righteous gasbag who couldn't follow direction, or one who is wisely obedient and knows his stuff. In other words, this was a moment in the spotlight to either shine or shit.

Regardless of the question, some guys couldn't help but frame the answer in the context of the backmasking scare, like a politician who uses a question as an opportunity to make himself look good, rather than answer the actual question. The list of rock bands and artists accused of backmasking continued to grow, as did the list of songs. We were constantly being barraged with thoughts about Satan and his evil influence. It got very tiresome, and distracting.

At one study, a young man read what must have been two or three whole verses of satanic tripe. The song was Led Zeppelin's *Stairway To Heaven.* Even if one believes there is a line or two here or there that sounds like a satanic message, how is it possible that the several complete verses that this young man quoted were of that sort?

They weren't. I proved to myself that they weren't.

In my room, I had a direct drive turntable. Most turntables are belt driven, mine was direct drive. It's very difficult to make a belt driven turntable play backward at a consistent speed. The speed can play havoc on the audio produced, so it's almost inconceivable that anyone with a belt-drive turntable could perform a viable experiment. Not so with my direct drive turntable. I played all of the main songs that were constantly in question backward at a consistent speed. Sure enough, almost none of the claims we were hearing had any truth to them. The exceptions are so few and far between that it's profoundly idiotic to presume that they are proof of occult goings-on.

Just to drive home the point, at some later date I modified a tape deck to play backward. I played some of Watchtower's

Bible tapes and recordings of Kingdom Songs with it. Most of the result was garbled gibberish, but enough questionable messages sneaked through so as to destroy the argument that backmasking is the domain of only rock musicians under Satan's influence. I don't remember which ones said what, it was so long ago and the battle so inconsequential. In writing this tome, however, I decided to take a few minutes to fiddle around with the abundant audio/video that is now available on the jw.org website.

With WAV editing software it only takes the press of one button to make any size audio file play backward perfectly.

In less than ten minutes, on the second audio I selected, I found a ringer.

Within the first minute of Anthony Morris' "Jehovah Will 'Carry It Out,'" talk, there is one segment where he seems to say, "I want to have fierce sex with you Betha."

It is somewhat garbled, but no more than the audio that had been used to prove that so many rock artists were in league with Satan.

One auspicious morning at breakfast, the Morning Worship

chairman, Karl Klein, brought to our attention some artwork created for one of the magazines by someone in the Art Department. The art in the magazines in those days was two-color, and appeared as drawings, whether they were based on a photograph or not.

When stared at long enough, the pattern in the dress of the woman in the picture began to appear as a menacing face. The critic(s) that had brought it to the attention of the GB thought it was the face of Satan. That was also the interpretation of many who started to look at it in order to verify the phenomenon. The implication was that the mixed-message picture was created that way deliberately, and apostasy was creeping into the Art Department.

Klein pointed out how inappropriate and unkind it is to question the spirituality and loyalty of the anonymous artist. This person was, after all, a faithful JW who was performing her Bethel work diligently and with sincerity. A real human being with feelings. He then compared the illusion to looking at clouds in the sky and seeing objects that morph into other objects – e.g. an elephant one second, a tree the next.

When I got to work that morning, everyone was, as usual, discussing what we had just heard. One of my co-workers, Alice LaFranca (wife of Pat LaFranca) correctly opined on how thoughtless it is to accuse a faithful sister of deliberately creating satanic imagery for the magazines, and restated Klein's comparison of the artwork to clouds.

In response, I agreed with her, but added that we have been more or less trained to think that way, considering all the foolish, conspiratorial talk of backmasking that was going on unabated.

Alice's facial expression turned at once sad and indignant, as she said, "You sound like the apostates," referring to the Bethel family members that had been disfellowshipped for apostasy in the last several years.

Reality can be pretty uncomfortable when one believes the mantra that everything in the world is from Satan, and everything from Watchtower is from God.

El Presidente

Somehow a rumor started in Westbury not long after our arrival at Bethel that I was working directly with Fred Franz, the President of Watchtower. My only guess is that it was because I had explained to someone that I was working in the Administrative Data part of the Computer Department, and that the chairman of the Administrative Data Committee (ADC) was Grant Suiter, Secretary-Treasurer and GB member. The next thing you know, word is that I'm working in the president's office. Even working with Suiter directly would not become a reality for a year or so, as I did no computer work with the Treasurer's Office at first, and it was a while before I was invited to any ADC meetings.

I cleared up that rumor pretty quickly and never heard it again.

I may have met Franz by the time of that rumor, but then again I may not have. Of course I finally did at least by the time the Gilead table foot position rotated to the letter "F."

I used to SEE him nearly every day since our second week at Bethel, as I did most if not all of the GB members. After all, we did work and eventually live in the same building (after we moved to the 5th floor of 124).

My memories of Franz are scattered, as he was often quiet and reserved. The anecdotes that follow are for the most part brief, and not connected with much else.

Franz lived in a modest, single-man room on the 8th floor of 124 Columbia Heights, very close to one of the libraries. His lifestyle was also modest. Although there was an unwritten rule that Bethelites under a certain age (different for men and women) should use elevators only if going up or down more than three stories, the blind and very short Fred Franz always walked anyway, often two steps at a time. He did that to and from his 8th floor room, his 10th floor office in the Executive Offices of 25 Columbia Heights, and everywhere else.

A semi-annual highlight of every year was the Gilead graduation. The Wednesday before the weekend event would be a special noon meal. We would have steak fillets or something else special that was reserved for just those occasions. We would all get off from work ten or fifteen minutes early in order to participate in a pre-dinner tradition. Many Bethelites would have others up to their rooms for hors d'oeuvres and possibly a glass of wine. It was up to the host to invite whomever they wished, or non-hosts to accept invitations as they wished.

At one Gilead meal, Franz was at our table. We had steak fillets. My main memory of that event was that he didn't eat any of his steak – he wrapped it up and took it home with him for a later time. It occurred to me that he did that because he was already blind by that time, and cutting the meat would be awkward, difficult, and perhaps embarrassing. I regretted not offering to cut it for him. C'est la vie.

The actual Gilead graduation was always Saturday afternoon. There would be many talks by various elite Bethelites, including GB members and Gilead school instructors. There would be skits put on by the graduates, which were sometimes quite humorous.

The highlight of all highlights was when the President, Fred Franz would deliver the main discourse of the day. His talk would invariably become a study article or two in a Watchtower later that year. We were always waiting for new light. It never arrived.

It takes great patience to listen to a laboriously technical speaker like Franz talk about what we used to believe, why it is now wrong, what we will now believe, and why that is right.

Use of Greek and Hebrew words would abound. We would hang onto every word with bated breath waiting for that elusive moment of enlightenment.

The one talk that I remember best was at the May, 1982 graduation ceremony, when Franz bellowed, "Carry on as MEN!" midway through the talk that bore that title. We nearly jumped out of our seats at the sound of his booming voice, especially on the word, "MEN!" We all talked about it for weeks and months. Damned if I could remember the point, though.

Franz' office was not any bigger or more ornate than mine or that of most others. One significant characteristic of its décor, however, was that, while Don Adams had Nathan Knorr's old furniture in his office, Franz had Rutherford's. Also, the entire wall behind him was a ceiling-to-floor, completely stocked bookcase.

Just two little stories about Franz that I always found amusing.

He used to regularly spend time in the pool and sauna above the basement laundry of 119 Columbia Heights. One time, while sitting with nothing but a towel to protect him, one of the young men who were sitting with him told the others that he had just got engaged to be married. Franz jumped to his feet, sans towel, raised his right arm, and shouted, "Hip hip hooray! Hip hip hooray!"

One morning I had breakfast in the Lower Dining Room for some reason that I don't recall. It's possible I was either among the panel of four Morning Worship commenters, was the text or yearbook reader, or said the prayer. Whatever the case may be, the chairman's talk was about how we should and shouldn't treat each other. Especially should we avoid picking on someone's weaknesses. He drove home the point with an illustration about chickens. A chicken will peck at another chicken and injure it either because it is already perceived as weak, or for some other unapparent reason. Other chickens will proceed to peck at the wound. Peck, peck, peck, until the victim finally dies of its wounds. We are not to contribute to a similar "pecking order" among us.

Franz was somewhere in that same dining room.

After Morning Worship and breakfast, by the time he walked near to the elevator, there was a long line of people waiting for it, mostly single young men. As Franz walked by them, he pointed randomly at each one of them, shouting, "Who's a pecker? Are you a pecker? Which one of you is a pecker?"

Of course nearly everyone got the vernacular meaning of the word, "pecker." Fortunately, Franz' outburst was intended and delivered as humor, so they didn't have to try too hard to suppress their laughs.

Pretty ironic that my last two stories about Franz more or less involve a certain male body part, don't you think? I wonder if Franz had any idea of what he was actually saying.

A word about Natheer Salih, personal assistant to Fred Franz in those days.

It has been stated on various websites and in various blogs, etc. that Natheer was Franz' body guard. Those same references explain that he is quite tall (6'2"or taller), and make all sorts of claims that range from inaccurate to just plain incorrect.

Natheer was not Franz' "body guard." He was his personal assistant, helping the blind Fred Franz navigate and accomplish things in a sighted world. If he were his bodyguard, how does one explain that of all the times I saw Franz (probably several times a week for years), I rarely saw the two of them together? Not much of a bodyguard, eh?

I don't know Natheer's exact height. I just know he is/was not tall. Maybe 5'7" or so? I know from standing next to him that he is quite a bit shorter than me. I am 6'2". And not blind.

One might as well figure that any article that contradicts those two simple facts is probably wrong about a lot more. Don't get me started.

Natheer is the brother of Mary Salih, whom I personally know as the matriarch of the Abrams family in Newton, New Jersey. I was in Sussex, the next nearest congregation to Newton. We were friendly and had many mutual friends with their son James.

Opening Up

Not long after the lectures about sexual immorality within the Bethel Family, another matter came up that, to me, was in a way more shocking. There is a certain amount of logic to why someone would opt for sex of any kind with any consenting adult. There has to be a reason why a very inefficient method of reproduction works so well and so often. That reason is that it's so damn pleasurable, so alluring, and so... great! If it could be bottled, it would put all the water companies, all the soft drink bottlers, and even all the alcohol manufacturers out of business.

What came up next in the rotation of no-guests-allowed special lectures to us idiots was a presentation on an unnatural, stupid, zero-benefit practice called, "opening up."

I had heard about it one day while walking through the Heights with Rick and his brother-in-law Tom N. Rick worked in construction. Tom was a floor overseer in the press room. It seemed that "opening up" was mainly practiced routinely by young, single men in those two departments. Rick bemoaned the practice as unchristian and pointless, while Tom's position was that it is, "just what press room guys do. It's neither wrong nor right. It just is." It took me a minute to begin to understand what they were talking about. After they cleared it up for me, I didn't feel enlightened or "in the know." I felt sick.

"Opening Up" is a type of hazing, performed mainly but not exclusively on newer recruits. The name comes from one of the principal manifestations of Bethel hazing.

A group of guys would gang up on one other guy, and get him to the floor. Several of them would keep him pinned down, with no ability to protect or defend himself, or escape. The others would pick one spot on his body, usually one of his pectorals, and viciously punch him in that spot with their bare knuckles. Each would take turns doing that over and over and over again. As was already mentioned, the victim had no ability to even cover the spot, because they were, "opening him up," keeping his arms away from his chest with nothing to hinder their ability to work that special spot. The area would become purple, distended, and of course extremely painful. At least one guy, who was unwittingly instrumental in exposing the whole thing, suffered broken ribs as a result.

The program that the GB developed used, as was the case with the sex program, only members of the GB. The difference this time was that only one talk was given, by one man. The others variously chaired the meeting and delivered the opening and closing prayers, but the lecture was delivered by Dan "The Man" Sydlik.

Dan was the obvious choice. He had been a boxer in years past. He was athletic. He knew how to rough house without getting inappropriate, and did so. He knew how to get down in the dirt with the young guys and help them have a great time, releasing their youthful energy healthfully. He spoke their language. And they respected and loved him like no other. No one had their ears like Dan did.

That night we learned that "Opening Up" goes beyond what was already described. Any kind of cruel beating that could be administered was on the table. No body part was off limits.

There were cases of young men being thrown into dumpsters. Dumpsters like the ones in the basement tunnel between the 124 and 107 buildings typically rose so far off the ground that one could not look over the top edge to see what was inside without climbing a ladder. Did those pranksters have any idea what might be in that dumpster, what the victim might be landing on? Broken glass? Protruding pieces of sharp metal?

In some cases, guys were thrown into running showers while fully clothed. That in itself might not seem so bad. Except when Dan pointed out that, "One brother was thrown into a running shower while wearing a brand new suit. That suit cost $150." [In today's money that is about $600.] "Who is going to pay for that suit??"

The young man with the broken ribs was known to us. He went to the Bethel Infirmary out of necessity. When asked how it happened, he offered some lame reason, like, "I fell." He was covering for his cronies (READ: abusers).

It was obvious to Dr. Lowell Dixon that something else was afoot. The investigating men informed the victim that if he didn't fess up, he would be sent home, with no possibility of being appointed in any congregational capacity. If he told them who did it, and other details, he MAY be able to stay.

He fessed up.

That opened up "Opening Up."

After that Monday night lecture, some seasoned Bethelites pointed out how they and/or their cronies were, years ago, involved with certain pranks. Like dropping water balloons out of Bethel home buildings on unsuspecting passers-by. When they were found out, they had to stand at the chairman's table at Morning Worship (in those days Knorr always presided there), and apologize to the entire family.

By the 1980s things had changed a tad. I can only imagine the lovely behaviors that may have been dreamed up since we left in the mid-1980s.

I Know Where You Live

I promised more about playing Liszt's *2nd Hungarian Rhapsody* on Family Night, and the interactions with Karl Klein.

The show that included the four pianists playing that piece on two pianos, also featured an interview with Karl and Margareta Klein. The week before those performances may be the first occasion wherein I spent time in a GB member's room.

Once rehearsals of individual skits and musical numbers were at a good enough level, rehearsals of the entire show took place. Since the Kleins were part of the show, at that point we heard their life story every time there was a rehearsal.

Karl was visibly overjoyed to be hearing our musical performance, because he was such a great music lover. Numerous conversations between him and me ensued.

The ice breaker was when I first asked him, "So you really like Liszt?"

"Oh I do, especially the *Hungarian Rhapsody,* but also *Liebestraum.* But I prefer classical to romantic."

"Funny, I usually prefer a lot of the romantic period over the classical. But I really love Mozart. I guess I would say I cut my teeth on Mozart. Some of my earliest learning included a lot of his sonatas. But I also learned a lot from listening to Tchaikovsky's *1st Piano Concerto in Bb minor.* I bought and studied the sheet music at one point."

"They say that Tchaikovsky sounded better than he wrote, and Brahms wrote better than he sounded. Tchaikovsky is wonderful, but I really love Schubert," Klein retorted, beaming as he built to the name, "Schubert."

"Schubert. Yeah, his life spanned the end of the classical period and the beginning of the romantic, almost the same years as Beethoven, who really ushered in the romantic period."

"Beethoven's romantic period pieces were often bombastic. Schubert was more subtle. I prefer Schubert even to Beethoven."

"I'll have to listen to more Schubert. About all I currently have in my record collection is his *"Unfinished" Symphony.* Maybe on a future Family Night we'll hear some of his lieder, and maybe some Mozart."

We went on for quite a while longer, I'm just recalling what I can remember, the best I can. I doubt all the words are exact.

The Kleins had the entire cast up to their room for a cast party the week before the performances. They excitedly filled in a lot of additional details about their life story that weren't included in the show. I learned a lot about Karl's frequent clashes with Joseph Rutherford. Apparently the old Prez felt Karl needed constant attitude adjustments, one time scolding him, "Watch out Karl. The Devil's after you!" It sounds to me like Karl was more of a victim of a cult than a future leader of one. He would get himself worked up into a bit of an excited state as he spoke, which made him harder to understand than he already was – he had a garbled way of talking. Some would say, "He sounds like he has a mouthful of marbles."

They lived in the Towers building, in one of the nicer rooms that had its own bathroom. Mind you, it was still a Bethel room typical of the time – no kitchenette, (an amenity that even low seniority US Bethelites might have nowadays), and just enough room for a small refrigerator. Some of those Towers rooms actually comprised a suite of two rooms: a small living room, and a separate bedroom. Their room was tastefully furnished. Of course there was nothing luxurious about it. The only room in all of US Bethel I have ever seen that one might begin to apply a word like "luxurious" to is Knorr's old room.

Bethel rooms are distributed in a bidding process. Room bids take place once a year. The entire family gets the Saturday of Room Bids off from work, and walks throughout each building in the Bethel Home complex, checking out every room they wish to that is up for bid.

A room comes up for bid when its occupants vacate it, either by leaving Bethel or by moving to another room.

New Bethelites and others that for some reason don't have a room as a result of a previous bid, (referred to as "on bid"), are assigned to a room that no one else currently has on bid. If someone else wins it in the next bid, they are moved to another room, whether they have won their next room on bid, or no one has it on bid.

That all means that once someone has a room on bid, they can stay in that room as long as they stay at Bethel, if they wish.

Room bid slips are provided by Bethel Office to write one's name on top, and select each available room one is interested in, in order of interest. Only rooms that are up for bid are allowed to be entered and walked through by whomever wishes to.

The bidding slips are processed by Bethel Office in the order of seniority. Those with the most years of cumulative full time service go first (including regular pioneering and so on). Whether someone is on the GB, or works in the bindery, the process is the same – years of full time service, not position, is the only factor.

That is how, one year during our residence, when long-deceased Nathan and Audrey Knorr's room came up for bid, a man named Victor Marcy won it. Marcy held no special position – I don't even recall where he worked. He was a nice enough, hardworking man, but not someone who would be considered a Bethel "heavy." Of all the bidders on Knorr's room, he had the most seniority, so he got the most coveted (according to some) room in the complex.

We also bid on Knorr's room, using my wife's paltry seniority that was at least greater than mine, knowing that winning that room was an extreme long shot. My reasoning was that if everyone with more seniority than us passed it up for whatever reason, there is a scintilla of a chance we might win it. Would it hurt to try? Of course not! There was no limit to the number of rooms one could bid on, so why not?

In order to bid on it, we of course wanted to see it first. It was by far the largest of all the Bethel rooms, even by today's standards. There has never been another one quite like it. But size isn't everything. There were actually some old touches that would have to be changed, at considerable expense to the occupant. For instance it had a curved liquor bar that was a permanent fixture, and took up most of the middle of the room. It was not hard to imagine some of the higher seniority bidders passing on it.

Most of the GB members lived in the Towers building in those days. The only exceptions that I am aware of were Gangas and Fred Franz, already discussed in previous chapters. Towers was the only building with a high ratio of rooms with a bathroom to those with no bathroom. It was also the only building with double rooms as far as I know, other than Knorr's room, already discussed.

The old *Live Forever* book contained a picture that used Dan and Marina Sydlik's elegantly furnished Towers room.

Leo Greenlees was the only single GB member who had a roommate. His room was a normal sized one in the Towers building.

Grant and Edith Suiter lived in a beautifully furnished room in the Towers building.

All of those mentioned actually lived lifestyles that ranged from austere to modest. If they were high up enough to have been provided a car by the "company," and they wanted one, it was from the same pool of Buick models that Circuit and District overseers drive. There were a small number whose positions at Bethel involved handling enough money, making enough major financial decisions, and interfacing with enough outside people of influence, that they often received gifts of cash, booze, dinners, trips and other perquisites. Still, they lived in the same modest rooms, ate the same food each day with the rest of the family, walked the same path to work each day, and worked the same if not more hours than everybody else (except for Saturdays). If there is anyone getting rich off of Watchtower, I sure don't know how they're hiding it.

Our first full week at Bethel included housekeeper training. Regardless of the work assignment we would receive the following week, we spent that first week shadowing a housekeeper in one of the Bethel Home buildings, and she (always a woman) would teach us how to make a bed the Bethel way, vacuum, clean mirrors, and so on. It had nothing to do with the possibility of being assigned as a housekeeper; it had to do with learning what they go through, hence how to basically clean our own rooms BEFORE they would come in each day to do a complete cleaning.

My training took place on an upper floor of the Towers building. One of the rooms I had to clean and observe being cleaned was that of Harold Dies, a single, elderly man who was overseer of Cost Accounting. It was a very small, single-man room, well less than 150 square feet. What was unusual about it was how ornately it was decorated. His closet stored quite a bit more than a naked closet could, due to an automated closet organizer system. What blew my mind was that he had a full size organ in his room. I already knew that such musical instruments were not allowed in Bethel rooms, since I had arrived with several guitars (one acoustic, two electric) and a

Music Man amplifier (the size of a Fender Twin Reverb for those who might know what that means). The guitars were allowed to be stored in our closet, but the amp was not allowed. An exception was made for Dies for reasons I can only guess at. He was a well moneyed man from before his Bethel days, who also drove an expensive car that he paid for with his own money. Who knows?

My housekeeper trainer then took me across the floor to the room of Dean Songer. She wanted to demonstrate what the opposite of Dies' room looked like. Songer's single-man room, about the same size as Dies', was furnished with only the minimum that Bethel would issue to those who didn't want to provide their own furniture: a single bed, a dresser, a desk with one chair, and a small bookcase. There was nothing on any of the surfaces except for an alarm clock. No pictures anywhere. His closet stocked just about what a man could wear in the space of a week or two, nothing more. It was so antiseptic I could barely breathe – like being in the Sahara desert.

If one recalls that Songer was one of the few Bethel heavies that objected to Family Night, one might now draw a conclusion as to the psychological category that produces that thinking.

Preserving the Sandbox

Ted Jaracz was as dispassionate a man as I have ever known. Everything he said or did was always by the book. The problem was and still is, he helped write the book.

The only leisure activity that Jaracz enjoyed, to my knowledge, was basketball. There was an indoor basketball court behind two doors (one secret) to the right of the 25 Columbia Heights lobby as one faced it when entering the lobby. Jaracz would spend some of his spare time there, playing with the young men. I always assumed his main interest in doing that was the sport itself. It's possible that he had an ulterior motive that had to do with the young men, but it would be speculative, therefore inappropriate, to assume that as fact.

At some point during his tenure on the GB, Jaracz became chairman of the Service Committee, which directs the Service Department. Letters written to congregations, bodies of elders, and traveling overseers almost always originate from the Service Department, unless they are directly from the GB.

Lloyd Barry, the man who had raised concerns to Knorr about Jaracz' appointment to the GB, was chairman of the Writing Committee, which directs the Writing Department. The Writing Department produces, not just magazines and books, but also material for various schools, including periodic elders' schools and the elders' handbook.

Sometime in the 1980s, and continuing into the 1990s, the magazines (mainly *Awake!*) began featuring articles about depression and various mental disorders. They spoke of professional mental health services in favorable terms, even saying that if someone is prescribed medications in the course of such treatment, they shouldn't be criticized for cooperating with their therapists/physicians and taking their medications. Elders not specifically trained and licensed in those professional areas were not to try their hand at offering similar help, but were to continue shepherding along with whatever professional treatment a person might be receiving. I had a large binder with copies of just those articles that I had amassed since starting to notice the positive trend. As a result of all of this, I also immersed myself in studies involving brain physiology, human emotions, depression, psychology, and related fields. In later years when I served as an elder, I used what I learned as part of my conduct with those in my care, but always heeding the advice to not wade into the position of diagnosing and/or treating them as if I were a licensed therapist. The point is that I am well aware that there were increasing degrees of openness toward psychiatry and related fields in those days. It was a real, albeit brief phenomenon.

Around the same time, information was being taught in elders' schools that recognized the phenomenon of repressed memories, most often but not exclusively with regard to sexual abuse. Judgment was not to be passed on whether there was any authenticity to such when expressed by a congregation member, but they were to be recognized and the member treated lovingly despite the claim that the elders probably lacked the expertise to verify. I recall making copious notes to that effect in my elder handbook, as we were always instructed to do.

Also in those days, higher education was not necessarily condemned. It was not really recommended, but neither was it condemned. I will present just one simple piece of evidence of that fact. We often read/heard instruction to the effect that, if a family member decides to pursue higher education, it's best if it can be done at a college or university close to home, so that the student can live at home and commute, rather than live on campus. Does that sound like direction that was totally outlawing higher education?

During that same general time, elder bodies received direction pertaining to accusations of pedophilia made against an appointed man. He was to be immediately removed, regardless of the veracity and/or outcome of the claim. A man who was actually guilty of pedophilia could NEVER be appointed again. Apparently it was recognized that pedophilia is an unusually sick crime, perpetrated by individuals for whom there is no known cure, and no amount of "scriptural counsel" can change that.

What came from the Writing Department was Lloyd Barry's domain.

On the heels of all of this was something quite different emanating from Ted Jaracz' Service Department. And since Jaracz outlived Barry by about eleven years, it is also telling that material from the Writing Department progressively clamped down on the more reasonable past treatment of the subjects mentioned.

What began as letters and Kingdom Ministry articles that seemed to contradict information from Writing, evolved into a change in direction of the Writing Department itself, as new GB members came in that were recommended and approved by Jaracz.

No more positive view of professional help for mental health issues. No more recognition of the reality of repressed memories. An increasingly tight, condemnatory view toward higher education. And most tellingly, a greatly relaxed treatment of pedophiles.

Watchtower's two-witness rule has always been the fly in the ointment that goes a long way toward allowing pedophiles to operate. And the warped interpretation of what constitutes confidentiality, combined with the desire to perpetuate the system of confession peculiar to Watchtower, both of which prevent the reporting of sexual crimes to authorities, have coalesced with the two-witness rule to create the perfect sandbox for pedophiles. Further direction from the Service Department, and later the Writing Department, only cemented the situation.

What eventually developed is multitudinous cases of appointed men who are pedophiles or were/are otherwise sexual abusers, either being appointed to positions of oversight, re-appointed, or never removed. Rank-and-file disfellowshipped pedophiles, upon reinstatement, are typically treated as normal humans (they are not), and are allowed access to not only young congregation members, but to members of the community at large due in part to the nature of the public ministry.

The war that had developed between Barry and Jaracz, who never liked each other, had achieved the status of permanent malignancy.

The more recent iron-fisted view toward higher education should come as no surprise when one considers that Barry had benefited from higher education, while Jaracz did not. But where did the insanely liberal treatment of pedophiles come from?

As already mentioned in the chapter, "My Second Circuit Overseer," Jaracz was a gay man. But that is not the only information that Barry had brought to Knorr's attention.

While Jaracz was overseer of the Australian branch, four young men (their ages not available) each separately brought forth charges of sexual abuse committed by Jaracz upon them.

Additionally, there have been other credible accusations of child sexual abuse against Jaracz. Pat Garza stated publicly on September 27, 2002 , from the 25 Columbia Heights Watchtower office building, that Jaracz sexually abused her as a child. Her personal writings describe the events in detail. Also around that time, two women who are mental health practitioners testified at a Mental Health Conference in Texas,

USA, that they were molested by Jaracz as young girls. Their reason for entering the mental health field was mainly due to that experience – they wanted to help others who have also been abused.

Being a gay man is not a crime. Being a person who desires underage boys and girls, and acting on those desires, is.

Is it any wonder that the man who committed those crimes would want to suppress them, rather than let them interfere with his thirst for power and control?

Another thing to consider is that the database of sex-related cases Watchtower began compiling in the 1990s was since either destroyed by Watchtower or so hidden that it had become inaccessible. Why? Who is in that database that Watchtower needs to hide? Could it be that Greenlees and Jaracz are in it?

How convenient that its disappearance occurred right at the time that the Australian Royal Commission demanded it. And how appropriate that it is connected with Australia, where Jaracz was branch servant.

Shootout at the Fantasy Factory

Bob Butler worked in Factory Dispatch, along with other men who also reported to Max Larson, including Richard Wheelock and Calvin Chyke.

One day I was asked by Bob to write a stand-alone program that would allow him to hit a button whenever Lloyd Barry needed certain information that he used to like to have with him for zone visits. All of the information could be culled from the Shipping and Inventory system on the System 38 that I spent many months working on when Tim Pappas was overseer of Domestic Shipping. It was an easy job that didn't take long to complete. If memory serves me it had to do with statistics on printed and distributed books, broken down by the various editions of those books.

That is all of the work I ever did for Barry, but it was Bob who requested it. So it was Bob whom I met with in the factory to go over specifications. And we briefly discussed it mid-project when I ran into Bob in a local store, where he was purchasing a bottle of Colt 45 Malt Liquor. (I have no idea what I went in there for. It was probably not to buy alcohol, as I already had all the stock I could afford on a Bethel "salary," provided gratis by a member of my Columbus Circle congregation who was a superintendent at one of Central Park West's luxury buildings. The residents, who included actor Mark Hamill and others, tipped him copiously every year at Christmas with expensive liquor and such. We spent many nights playing cards and drinking the free scotch with Gary K and other Bethelite friends. Those nights always reminded me of the cover to the Kenny Loggins's album, "With Jim Messina Sitting In." We'd play that record as well as Neil Young, etc. Good times. How's that for a tangent? Can you believe my editor allowed this to slip past her?)

Of all the men in Factory Dispatch, the one I knew very well was Calvin Chyke.

Cal was an elder in my congregation, Columbus Circle, along with Don Underwood (worldwide construction overseer), Bill Hunkins (electric shop), and several local men. He and his wife Zelda were also in my book study that met Sunday mornings.

For the first year or so of our Brooklyn Bethel sojourn, we had no car. That meant we either had to ride the NYC subway system, or in the car of any Bethelite that might own one. After a short time of depending upon the subway system, it was requested that we ride with the Chykes in their car.

The Chykes' car ride team was a revolving door, as all of the young men that used that means of conveyance eventually came up with some lame excuse to not participate anymore. That because it was very uncomfortable riding with the Chykes. They were very old-school, conservative, by-the-book "company" people who could not resist spouting their views that were invariably judgmental, and counter to the way many young Bethelites think. Apart from the fact that Zelda liked to play football in Central Park with the young guys once in a while, neither of them endeared themselves to anyone.

A responsibility of the young men that rode with them was walking Cal back to the Bethel home from his parking spot on the ground floor of building #1 of the 117 Adams Street factory complex. It was about a ten minute walk. Given the state of affairs in New York City through the 1970s and 80s, it was a dangerous walk to be undertaking after 10:00 PM, the time we'd typically be getting home from the Kingdom Hall which was near 100th Street on Central Park West. The young men would take turns walking Cal home. None of us objected because of any safety concerns – we just didn't like walking with him, because it meant being alone with and talking to him.

I never actually minded the job much. I always felt that I could probably learn something from this older man who grew up in Pennsylvania during a time of fierce persecution of JWs that was also common in New York State and New Jersey.

One fateful evening, I did indeed learn something from Cal. Something that was quite disturbing. Something that had to do with putting Watchtower business way above an unfortunate "worldly" person's welfare.

The Adams Street factory complex sat right at the base of the stairway to the nobly picturesque Brooklyn Bridge. On this particular evening, Cal as usual parked his car, we got out, and after closing the garage door, started walking past the factory entrance and across the road near the bridge entrance.

We were confronted by a man who pleaded for our help. He had been riding his bicycle on the wooden path above the roadway deck, which path had separate lanes for bicycles and pedestrians. Now on the street at the base of the bridge, he was struggling to control his bike as he walked while also helping a seriously injured man who was only able to hobble along clumsily because he was being held up by the erstwhile cyclist.

The cyclist explained that he didn't know the wounded man,

but saw him being attacked by a robber who smashed his head with a tire iron or some similar heavy metal object. There was no reason to doubt his story, as the wounded man's head was clearly split open and bleeding profusely.

The cyclist had seen us exiting the garage and therefore assumed we could help.

Frantically, he pleaded, "Could you please help me get this man to the hospital? He was attacked on the bridge."

Cal responded haltingly, "Does he want to go the hospital?"

"Of course he does. I mean, he can't hardly talk, but of course he needs to get to the hospital."

Then, speaking directly to the wounded man, Cal asked, "Do you want to go to the hospital?"

It was a bit difficult to distinguish precisely what the wounded man said between the moans and gurgling sounds he was making. But I'm pretty sure he wanted to get to a hospital. Quickly.

Cal continued, "Did you try calling an ambulance?"

In the early 1980s people did not carry cell phones. The cyclist looked incredulously at Cal, as if he could muster neither of the only two words that could possibly be the answer to such a dumb question.

I asked Cal desperately, "Can't we at least go into the lobby and call an ambulance?"

"The lobby is closed."

It didn't take long for the cyclist to realize that more time was being wasted on this foolish conversation than it was worth.

To this day I have no idea whether they ever made it to a hospital or not.

What I do know, thanks to Cal, is a more detailed understanding of the liability that could have been created for Watchtower had we got involved. That was the gist of our ensuing ten minute conversation.

I felt a special kind of sick in my gut that night. The story of the Good Samaritan came to mind. Guess which side of the story we were on.

A Few Good Men

I have tried to be as honest and even-handed as possible in relating the accounts in this tome. I will not create dirt where there is none. As has already been said in "Saint George The Owl," I personally don't believe that all the men who have ever served on the GB have been bad men who were deliberately running a cult. In fact I believe that the majority of the men I knew during my years at Bethel were well-motivated, albeit imperfect. As Ray Franz said, they were "victims of victims." Even when a man has apparently been guilty of gross sins that reveal great duplicity and hypocrisy by them as well as among the top brass, I have more or less left the conclusion of how to judge the man up to the reader.

Now I will talk about several more men about whom I can't think of anything critical to write.

My favorite of all of those men has to be Jack Barr.

John Barr (always called Jack) hailed from Scotland. Like many of the other GB members, I primarily got to know him at the breakfast and dinner table. But Barr also was one of the frequent visitors to our congregation who would give talks.

Barr had a sincerity about him that was unmistakable. Being one of the mildest men I have ever met, he also paradoxically would become quite passionate when referencing the Bible in his talks. His simplicity somehow inspired me to realize that imitating the example of Jesus was not the daunting task I so often felt it had to be – I wanted to be a better man, and it should actually be pretty easy to accomplish that.

His wife, Mildred, would often tell us that before they married many years ago, she told him that she wanted a husband that would read the Bible to her every day. And that is what Jack did.

Barr was always kind to me. Sometimes when I interacted with him, he would be otherwise concerned with some papers in his hands. He would turn his head upward, and with sincere love in his eyes, break into the tenderest smile that would make me wonder whether he was a little boy looking up at his Daddy (me??), or the older man that he obviously was, proudly looking up at his grandson (me!).

One day on the way to my office, I was apparently walking

quite slowly yet laboriously, feeling the weight of the spirit-sapping Columbus Circle congregation the morning after a typically discouraging meeting. I didn't realize how obvious my cluttered walk must have been to any one observing, until a man came up behind me, put his arm around me, and asked if everything was okay. It was Jack Barr.

All I remember saying was, "Yeah, thanks. I'm just kinda tired."

Jack knew better than to accept that lame response. He said in his reassuring, fatherly way, "If it's your body that's tired, you can always get more rest. If it's your spirit that's tired, you need something different."

There wasn't time to talk any further, so we both agreed to take it up at a later time. As it turned out, Jack's kind gesture was all that I needed at the moment.

The next time I saw Jack in the dining room, I just smiled and sort of winked. He smiled back. He knew what I meant, and I knew what he meant.

I am forever grateful for the privilege of knowing such a

beautiful man.

My wife was uncustomary absent from the dining room table one day at lunch. She might have been playing softball with the guys. I just know it had nothing to do with working overtime, which happened relatively often in the Laundry where she worked.

The Barrs were at our table. Mildred asked me where my wife was.

I took one sentence to explain.

Mildred proceeded to chastise me, in as modest a way as she could muster, for allowing my wife to miss lunch at the Bethel table. Some of her words were directed at my absent wife. She explained that back in the day, when she was a member of the Bethel family in London, missing lunch was unheard of.

She then went on to explain how there was also a curfew that mandated everyone was to be home by a certain hour each evening, somewhere between 8:00 PM and 10:00 PM. The doors would be locked so that there was no way to get inside.

What would happen to a hapless Bethelite that missed the curfew by so much as a fraction of a minute, I don't know. I was just glad that brand of draconian rule was too long-gone to matter anymore. Besides, we were living in Brooklyn, not London.

John Booth was an enigma to me. I don't know what he actually did as a member of the GB. He may have been on the Personnel Committee. I don't recall any of his talks, even as chairman at Morning Worship. But here he was, an esteemed member of the supreme elder body of the JW organization.

What I do know is that this man who was most comfortable in a flannel shirt was genuinely humble. When he interacted with younger women, usually accompanied by their husbands, he displayed a genuine interest in what they had to say, almost to the point of falling over his words.

One morning while walking from the Bethel home to the office building, Booth was talking more to Roger T than me, but I overheard the conversation well. (Remember the man that arranged for Liszt's *Hungarian Rhapsody* on Family Night? That was Roger T.)

Roger asked Booth how he was doing. Booth usually walked hunched over and had a rather uninspiring demeanor and appearance. But something about his body language that day made him appear to be discouraged about something.

"How are you today, Brother Booth?"

"Oh, not s'bad, thanks."

"Good to hear. I thought you seemed a little preoccupied for a minute there. Must be my eyes."

"Oh well, sometimes it just seems like it's hard to do the right thing even when you know what's right. I just don't know sometimes..."

Roger spent the rest of the relatively long walk in a role reversal, bolstering the man he had so much respect for.

Martin Pötzinger was another outwardly simple man who did I-know-not what on the GB. But we tended to idolize him and his wife Gertrude because they were Nazi concentration camp survivors.

Early in Hitler's reign as chancellor of Germany, young Martin and Gertrude married. Almost immediately they were hauled away to separate concentration camps. They thereby spent the first nine years of marriage completely separated from one another, not even knowing if they would ever come out alive and see each other again.

Observing those two together was sweet, almost to the point of embarrassment. He doted on her like no other husband ever has. I recall one day, when Gertrude wasn't at the table due to illness, he gathered something from the table for her – I think it was scallions, but that must be a false memory, because, I mean, why scallions? I just can't imagine what else it might have been, but he grasped and carried them as if they were cut flowers, picked especially for his love.

The enthusiastic smile on his face said that they were flowers, so that is how I remember them, even though they certainly were not. I do recall wanting to offer some wisecrack, like, "Are those flowers for your wife, Brother Pötzinger?" Fortunately I controlled myself, but my honest memory is one of confusion – were they flowers, scallions, or something else?

Sometimes on a weekend afternoon I would see Martin and Gertrude doing street work, usually at the Clark Street subway station, but also at other locations on Montague Street. Possibly because of their lack of facility with English, and their thick German accents, they didn't talk much – rather they just beamed from ear to ear while holding up the magazines.

The release of the third film in the Star Wars series, *Return of the Jedi*, led to Pötzinger giving one of the most memorably comical discourses in all my time at Bethel.

In common with what was discussed in relation to the movie, *E.T. The Extra Terrestrial*, a number of young men went to see *Return of the Jedi* the day of its release, to ensure they would see it before the Morning Worship chairman had a chance to condemn it. The first showing was at midnight. Somehow the guys got home by 3AM, and made it to work on time the next day.

When the subject of the Star Wars movie did come up at Morning Worship, Pötzinger was the chairman.

Somehow he made the segue from a topic that had nothing to do with movies, Sci-Fi Fantasy, or The Force, to that very subject.

His discourse was so confusing and indiscernible that my only takeaway, indeed the only memory of it for most if not all of the family, was when he said in his heavy German accent:

"Vut is dis Jedi? I don't know dis Jedi. Do you know dis Jedi? Vut is dis Jedi?"

If he said it once, he said it five times.

Not exactly one of the more scintillating talks I've heard. But definitely one of the more entertaining.

Grant Suiter had a fall in his bathtub one morning that left him virtually paralyzed and in great pain. My sense was that it was a stroke that caused his fall, but we will likely never know for sure. Evidently he was not able to speak either. For many months he would give direction to someone from his bed as to financial and other decisions related to his work as Secretary Treasurer.

Soon after his inevitable death in 1983, Lyman Swingle was appointed to replace him as Secretary Treasurer.

Swingle had a very gruff appearance and demeanor. His mad scientist eyebrows only enhanced that impression. He spoke rather laboriously and cleared his throat often, which made it difficult to muster the patience to wait for his next delivery of droll sarcasm. His sometimes rough language would come out when, for example, calling another driver on the road an "asshole."

For all of Swingle's gruffness, Ray Franz speaks glowingly of him in his book, *Crisis of Conscience,* as someone who was kind and reassuring to Ray, and open to change as to GB policies and the treatment of others.

Like Pötzinger was to his wife Gertrude, Swingle was very sweet and loving to his wife, Crystal. I recall him being genuinely dismayed when she was missing from the dining room due to illness. It seemed to affect everything he said and did. One of us, noticing her absence, would ask him how she was, and there was sadness in his face and voice when he answered us. When he was chairman at Morning Worship and she was ill, he would include her in his public prayer quite tenderly.

One day at an ADC meeting that Swingle of course chaired, someone brought up the subject of combining the congregation account statement for the New York Corporation with the congregation account statement for the Pennsylvania Corporation. I quickly realized that it was probably a question for the Legal Department. I didn't think it was possible to combine the two legally. Nevertheless the matter was bandied about for what seemed like half the day.

Vernon Wisegarver in particular talked seemingly without an end in sight about that and everything else he thought should be changed while we're at it. I have never heard such a long, tiresome speech in all the business meetings I've ever been in, including one with Donald Trump as a guest speaker. (Don't get too excited, the Trump meeting was with so many people that The Don and I never actually met - I was just another audience member. It was a business pep-rally type of meeting, long before he got into politics.)

It may have been Judah Schroeder who finally vocalized my initial thoughts. Whoever it was, Swingle just acted as if Wisegarver had said nothing, and said, "Well, let's send the question up to the Legal Department. Anything else?"

That was Swingle's way of tactfully saying, "Enough of this gasbag. Now let's get down to business."

I always thought that the logical heir to Knorr's throne was his assistant, Milton Henschel. That transition didn't happen until the death of President Fred Franz in December 1992.

Henschel was in his early twenties when he was selected by Knorr as his assistant.

A very quiet man, he is probably the most mysterious to me of all the GB members. I don't recall any interactions with him apart from saying Good Morning and so on. What I do remember is that every morning he would spend all of the time at the table before breakfast was served (about twenty minutes) working and massaging his massive hands with each other. John G, one of the Gilead students, was the only one who had the nerve to ask him why he did that. It was essentially due to arthritis.

Henschel was actually one of the most boring speakers I've ever heard. That doesn't mean I had a bad opinion of him or dreaded his talks. It was just kind of boring.

My only significant memory of him was from an event I did not attend, but one of my workmates related the story to me.

Dave T not only worked with me in the Computer Department, but he was also a ventriloquist. One of the things I learned from Dave is that ventriloquists can get away with a lot if their potentially offensive comedy is said by (through) their dummy.

Dave was invited to entertain at a party that included some GB members and other Bethel heavies. Milton and Bun Henschel were there. Henschel was quite tall, and bald-headed. It is no mystery why he was thought of as Daddy Warbucks. It's just that I don't think anybody ever told him that to his face. That is, not until Dave T and his dummy.

Dave went right up to Henschel, who was seated, and launched joke after joke at him through his dummy about his baldness, and his likeness to Daddy Warbucks. Henschel loved the entire routine and couldn't stop laughing.

Now just imagine little ol' me doing the same thing to Henschel at the breakfast table.

Hairy Carey

"Pretty good when you add it all up."

That was Carey Barber's only comment to the Bethel family at Morning Worship after reading a brief report of what "apostate" Ray Franz was now up to in his Alabama home.

It would be about ten years later that I would finally have the opportunity to speak to Barber in private about Ray.

I first met Carey and his wife Sydney at the Gilead table for breakfast one Monday morning in 1981. I asked Sydney about her work.

"Where do you work, Sister Barber?"

"I work in the offices."

"Oh, so do I. In the Computer Department. Administrative

Data, on the 5th floor. Not publishing, which is on the 6th floor. What department do you work in?"

"I work in Indexing."

"Indexing. I've heard about Indexing. But I don't know what it is. What do you do there?"

"Indexing. I work with indexing."

"Yes, but what do you actually do?"

"Well, you know what an index is, don't you?"

"Yes, of course. But there are many kinds of indexes, and many things that can be indexed. I was just wondering…"

It suddenly became clear to me that Indexing was a big secret, and this nebulous conversation was going to stay that way. The subject was changed to something else.

We learned what Indexing was all about no later than 1984, when the *Reference* edition of the *New World Translation of the Holy Scriptures* was released. The department had been working on the footnotes and center column cross-reference apparatus. That was the big secret. I can't imagine the need for or benefit of ultimate confidentiality, but there you have it.

One time when I was assigned to answer a question at the Family Watchtower study, Barber was conducting. My question had a very simple answer, nothing that could be elaborated on at any appreciable length. So, even though we were allotted one minute per answer, and serving on the Watchtower study panel was every young Bethelite's moments to shine, I took only a fraction of that time. I just couldn't see the point of blowing a lot of wind in order to impress the family with my supposed erudition and research skills.

Barber had already been showing subtle signs of senescence. Now, during the Watchtower study, he was clearly unfocused.

Bethel Family Watchtower conductors don't typically ask a lot of auxiliary questions. But Barber decided to ask me one, evidently because he realized my answer could have been longer, and perhaps because he felt there was more to say. There was not. The question he asked me was almost the same as the printed question for the next commenter, the "b" question. Recognizing that, I did my best to add some more meat without stepping on the next commenter. Barber appeared confused, either because my answer was odd, or because he began to realize his mistake. He fumbled for a moment, then turned to the next comment and asked the "b" question.

It was a simple mistake, one that I don't think needs to be made an issue of. Anyone can make a mistake like that. I'm just writing about it because it was a lesson to me on how to innocuously do the right thing and show respect at the same time.

The next morning at work, a couple of the guys as usual made some conversation about the study. They had all noticed Barber's gaffe, and commended me for the brevity of my initial answer, and for not embarrassing Barber in front of the whole family.

At least it all ended right. No need to fret about the possibility that the unforgivable sin had been committed by botching a Watchtower answer.

In 1992, a brand new Kingdom Hall was completed for the Sussex, New Jersey congregation. Gabe C and I were the only elders not intimately involved in the construction effort. Gabe was too old at that point. Since my construction experience consisted mainly of weekend warrior projects around my own house, and all the other elders had more experience, I was selected to conduct many of the Watchtower studies, the Theocratic Ministry School, give the occasional Public Talk, service meeting parts, and so on. I don't know to what extent the congregation got tired of seeing me on the platform, but I do know that I pined for the day when I could actually spend a few minutes PREPARING for some this stuff, when I could actually do the parts and the audience justice.

The day came for the dedication of the new Kingdom Hall. Carey Barber was assigned to perform the dedication. That included the special talk and dedication on Saturday evening, and a full Sunday program as well. Barber stayed with me and my family at our house on New York Avenue in Sussex.

In preparation for his visit, I asked a few Bethelite friends who knew him on a more personal level what his likes and dislikes are. I was told that a bottle of good quality scotch would be a very good idea. So I bought a bottle of fifteen-year-old Dimple Pinch, a pleasure I had recently discovered at a gathering with some friends in Lindenhurst, Long Island.

Subsequent to that, I spoke to Sydney on the phone. I don't recall whether she called me or if I had called her. She informed me that she would not be able to accompany her husband. She wanted me to know that a quiet, peaceful weekend with not too many people around was best for him, and please not too much rich food and no booze.

As much as I planned on respecting Sydney's wishes, I was also determined to let Carey decide what he wanted to do. As it turned out, Sydney's wishes were not ignored, but not followed either.

I drove alone to Brooklyn Heights to pick up Barber. When we got to my car that was parked in front of 119 Columbia Heights, I noticed that a double-parker had blocked us in. Barber got in the car anyway, and I just made some sort of lame effort to find the inconsiderate owner of the offending vehicle.

While we were waiting, a Bethelite whom I knew walked by and, noticing Barber in my car, said, "Looks like you've got quite the dignitary in your car."

Just then, another person who happened to be walking by overheard us, stopped and stared, and asked, "Who? Who?"

New Yorkers are used to seeing celebrities at times, especially in neighborhoods like Brooklyn Heights, where Art Carney and Norman Mailer lived, Robert Redford and others frequently dined, and Paul Newman, Farley Granger and others filmed movie scenes. And with the United Nations just a couple of miles north, by the East River, it actually could have been virtually anyone from anywhere in the world in my car.

Realizing the passerby was probably not a JW, I clumsily explained that my passenger was an executive at Watchtower. In a split second, the passerby registered a look of disgust, turned and walked away.

New Yorkers seldom measure distance in miles. They measure in time. The literal distance has no meaning, as a one mile trip can take an hour, the same as a thirty mile trip. The drive from Brooklyn Heights to my home in Sussex is typically a two hour drive, but could be a little less or a lot more. What is it in miles? Fifty? Sixty? Who knows?

Barber and I had plenty of time to talk during that drive. At some point the conversation turned to the subject of Ray Franz. But please allow me to save that for last. First you want to hear about the weekend, right?

Saturday afternoon, my then-wife took Barber to visit a friend who was in the hospital due to a bite from a brown recluse spider. I don't know whether Lisa C, in her state of delirium, fully realized who Barber was, but my wife reported that he very tenderly cupped her face in his hands, smiled very close to her face, and offered some words of encouragement.

Later he sat in on my wife's study with Judy K. I'm nearly certain that my wife conducted the study, but it's possible that I'm wrong. (Sometime later, I created a video of the construction project and dedication weekend that included a picture of the three of them during that Bible study. I also got a few nice pictures of Barber with my three young kids.)

All that I remember about Barber's dedication talk is that he talked a little about how the Society's work is funded, and said that he would talk about it more tomorrow (Sunday). On both occasions, all he talked about was little kids donating small change and scraps of things that had no intrinsic value. Something tells me there's a bit more going on than that.

After the dedication program, we had some people over the house for some snacks and conversation. I don't remember how many or who was there, mainly because any social plans were always bloated by the time my wife finished extending the list of invitees to half the planet.

I always had a pretty good stock in my liquor cabinet. Stoli vodka, Tanqueray gin, Jim Beam bourbon (my favorite since a CO turned me onto it), Guyanese or Barbadian rum, maybe some tequila, various wines, and a few liqueurs. Nobody ever got drunk at my house, but the booze was always available to anyone of legal age.

Contrary to Sydney's wishes, Carey enjoyed the scotch with us.

Among the plethora of hors d'oeuvres was an assortment of crackers, cheese, salami and other toppings. Barber made one for himself that also included onion strings. He had so many of the little canapés that I couldn't count. Since the onion strings tended to look like hair dangling off of the mountain of condiments on his cracker, we called it a Hairy Carey.

We all had tons of laughs and fun. What Sydney would never know would never hurt her. Or Carey. At least I don't think so.

After Sunday's meeting the following the day, I took Barber to a restaurant in Chester, New York that was billed as a clam house. Bob S, our PO, joined us for the meal and the ride back to Brooklyn while our wives were occupied with something else. Before we left my house to pick up Bob, Barber and I were standing alone in my kitchen with our coats on, when he looked at me and sheepishly and slowly asked, "Are we... gonna have... another... nip?"

I responded, "You mean of Scotch?"

"Is that OK?"

"Oh yeah, I mean, sure. Yes. I guess we have a minute before we have to pick up Bob."

So we had another nip before dinner.

During the ride to Brooklyn, I turned the conversation in such a way as to demonstrate to Bob that we in the Sussex congregation had become major rule makers without the authority to do so. Sussex was a sort of insane asylum, with rules about going to the conventions we're assigned to, what to do about people who break that rule, how members of the opposite sex must conduct themselves, and an enormous litany of things that boggled the mind. Bob was originally from Verona, a more sophisticated part of New Jersey. But still, he was stuck between a rock and a hard place with the bullying and small-town nonsense that was going on within the elder body.

One example was of a single man in his late twenties who had been recommended as a Ministerial Servant. When the approval came back from the branch and he was informed of it, he informed the elders that he felt guilty about accepting because he was having difficulty with the habit of masturbation. (Somehow I instinctively knew that did not mean he needed instructions, but that he was having difficulty kicking the doggone habit.) The elders instantly removed him, revoked all other privileges, and in general treated him like a pariah.

I asked Barber if he felt that we had gone too far.

He said, "Yes, there's no need to treat him that way. You'll crush his spirit if you do that."

I already knew that. I wanted Bob to hear it.

Shaking his right hand with both of mine in the lobby of the Towers building was the last time I ever saw Barber. He died in 2007.

That's all I've got to say about Carey Barber. Or is it? Am I forgetting something? Oh, yes I promised I would talk about Ray Franz.

During the two hour drive from Brooklyn Heights to Sussex, I explained to Barber why I never read any of Raymond Franz' *Crisis of Conscience.* It was not because I thought it would poison my mind. I always knew that if I had "the truth," it and my own mind should be strong enough to defend against any contrary teaching. There was one simple reason.

"I figure that, if Ray recounts anything about conversations in Governing Body meetings or with others, I would have no way to verify whether what he says is true or false. Who is going to ever tell me what actually happened if it's that confidential? So I might as well be reading the National Enquirer on line at the grocery store."

Barber countered, "Ray talked a lot. One time during a Governing Body meeting, he talked for so long that Grant Suiter finally interrupted and said, 'You know Ray, you sure talk a lot.' Grant said what we were all thinking, but I don't think Ray ever got it or took it to heart. He liked to hear himself talk."

I responded, "I never met Ray. I came to Bethel in fall of 1981, and he was gone sometime earlier that year. But I do remember the family in general having nothing but bad things to say about him after that article in Time magazine... actually after the announcement about him."

"Jehovah has a way of bringing things to light. It was a difficult time but in the end it all works out."

I recalled, "It was described by some as a sort of heaviness. As if the Holy Spirit was being grieved. Work was difficult. I remember the Kingdom Ministry in the late 70s or 1980 mentioning... That reminds me, it was Ray that changed Kingdom Ministry to Our Kingdom Service, wasn't it?"

"He was always trying to de-emphasize the importance of the ministry. Talking about word meanings and saying we're not ministers."

"Man. So tricky. So subtle and so tricky. Somehow he was able to convince even other Governing Body members of his ideas."

"Oh, he had nobody fooled. Nobody went along with his ideas."

"I'm sure. But to get the word "Ministry" removed from the title of a publication? He couldn't have done that by himself."

"Why not?"

"Well, I mean he would have to explain to the whole Service Committee why it should be changed. They would have to agree. It would affect the whole Service Department. All the Section Men. Even the printers in the factory would have adjustments to make. It's a pretty big thing."

"Not every word is approved by committee. It's possible, while not likely, that a letter can go out from the Service Department with a mistake in it."

"Yes, but this was every month for years. The name of the publication was changed."

"Jehovah only let it go so far. It was a test for his people."

After thinking about that for a moment, I replied, "I guess that means anyone that wasn't disfellowshipped for apostasy repented."

"Not necessarily. Everyone was given the opportunity to repent. Nobody repented, so they were all disfellowshipped. When Jehovah cleans house, he cleans house."

"But I mean, nobody else on the Service Committee was disfellowshipped. Hardly anybody in the Service Department was disfellowshipped as far as I know."

"Because they weren't involved."

"OK. But again I go back to the fact that none of his proposed changes could have been adopted in a vacuum. Others had to know what was happening and even approve some of it. It could easily have been prevented."

There was silence for a minute or so.

Finally, I restarted the conversation by saying, "Believe me, I have no sympathy for Ray Franz, or any other apostate for that matter. I just always found it disturbing that it seemed OK for anyone to characterize his every conversation as packed with lies. Meanwhile he was on the Governing Body. I mean, if he was that bad, what was the holdup?"

Barber closed that aspect of the conversation by saying, "Like I said, Ray talked a lot."

I took that as code that I was now talking too much. About a subject I should not be trying to analyze.

We had just passed the United Nations building. Although it is not visible from the FDR Drive roadway, we both knew we were passing under it. The conversation turned to Gilead School and the part of the training that includes a trip to the UN.

The subject of Ray Franz never came up again.

Mister Manners... er, Moneybags Again

Grant Suiter lived as modestly as anyone else at Bethel. Almost. He did have a "company" car, which was an option for any GB member and certain others. But it was just a Buick, the same as any traveling overseer. The room in Towers that he and his wife Edith lived in was very nicely decorated and had a bathroom, but was not much bigger than others like it.

He did however have a fairly dapper appearance. His suits always seemed to be of somewhat higher quality than average – maybe it was just the way they hung on him, or the way he walked. His shoes were beautifully polished. And he often wore a designer hat.

One day, when he was Morning Worship chairman, he made the following the announcement: "A man's brand new, rather expensive black hat, size [x], has gone missing from the coat closet above the 4th dining room in the 124 building. If anyone knows of its whereabouts, please return it to its owner. It has the initials "GS" on the inside of the brim."

There is no doubt Suiter was able to enjoy a modest amount of finer things due to his outside connections. "Green handshakes" are common among traveling men and Bethel brass. Occasionally persons have even taken men like him on a shopping spree to buy a suit or what have you. One of the best kept secrets was that there was always at least one bottle of booze in the Treasurer's Office safe. I confirmed that when I was once invited to have a drink for some special occasion that I don't recall. It might have been the 100th anniversary of the opening of the Brooklyn Bridge.

There was a man we called Mr. Coffee who lived somewhere in Brooklyn. He would come to the Bethel complex four or five days a week, usually starting on Tuesday or Wednesday. He would spend the entire morning, from 6:00 AM or earlier until about lunch time standing in front of the various buildings, spouting rhetoric that was against Watchtower, its workers (the Bethelites), and especially the men who were on the judicial committee that had disfellowshipped him.

He was called Mr. Coffee because one of his criticisms was that we were all drug addicts because we always drank coffee. He also had a problem with the color black (because coffee is black?). At one point he attached white paper to his otherwise black "service bag" brief case with paperclips in order to not have the color black associated with him.

Mr. Coffee had a special hatred for Suiter, who may have been on his judicial committee along with Mario Zulo and one other elder, either Richard Wheelock or Max Larson. Every morning, when he spotted Suiter walking from the home to his office (always with Edith on his right arm), he would walk up behind him and spit vitriol at him. Sometimes some of the young men would form a buffer around the Suiters to keep Mr. Coffee at bay. I was among that number once or twice.

Regardless of what happened, one thing was the same each morning. Suiter never responded to Mr. Coffee in any way. He didn't bat an eye, didn't look at him, didn't retaliate, and didn't call the police – he just took the abuse and made his way to his office.

Every Bethelite was issued a tear-sheet once a year. It consisted of the Daily Texts for each day of the year, three on each side of each piece of paper. When a sheet was completed, one would simply tear it off and throw it away.

When Suiter's sheet was finished, he would always practice some elementary origami with it. Usually a paper airplane. He would then hand it to someone at the table. Now what would you do with a paper airplane someone just handed to you? Its only purpose is to fly. But what sensible young Bethel man is going to launch a paper airplane in the Bethel dining room, at Grant Suiter's table? Well, my wife would. She threw it directly at Suiter, hitting him front and center.

The young guys reacted with shock, waiting in dread to see what would happen next.

Nothing happened. Except that after a few seconds, Suiter laughed.

That would never have happened if it were a male playing the trick. The same Grant Suiter who would chastise someone for sneezing or blowing their nose at the table, would not put up with it. Licking one's fingers after eating chicken or ribs was another no-no. In fact, there were a lot of no-no's that Suiter would gladly point out to anyone who would transgress in his presence. Mister Manners he was.

I was told by my good friend Gary S (the real estate attorney) that Suiter was at one time very funny and quick witted, but that as the years passed so did his ability to tell jokes. His repertoire get very out of date, with no new jokes coming in to replace the old ones.

One day Suiter made one of his occasional pop-ins to my office. Sometimes he would just pass through, cheerfully waving. Other times he would hang around for a bit, chatting away for a while. On this particular day, he left after saying, "This is a nice office. And the people aren't s'bad either." We all chuckled. Not two weeks later, after lunch on a Friday, the last day he would be at our table for another fourteen weeks, he said, "This is a nice table. And the people aren't s'bad either."

John G, the Gilead student at our table, said in his starchy manner, "Isn't it marvelous how our heavenly father has blessed us with a sense of humor?"

Now that cracked me up. I couldn't bring myself to force a laugh at Suiter's cute but tired joke. But the effect that ridiculous sentence emanating from the mouth of a two dimensional cardboard suit from Gilead school had on me was too much to hold in. I think Suiter may have thought that my laughter was a direct reaction to his superb joke. I dunno, but whatever works.

Whenever I had a meal with the Suiters that included a cup of tea, and I mean EVERY time, Edith would make the same remark. She'd say, "Oh, you're a teetotaler." I didn't have the heart to explain that "teetotaler" has nothing to do with drinking tea. Maybe she already knew that. Again, I dunno.

During the time that Suiter was incapacitated and even after his death, for some reason I often wound up at the same dining room table with Edith, mainly for supper. The conversation with others at the table would invariably include the ubiquitous question, "Where are you from?" My answer was always, "I'm from Long Island."

Each time, Edith would then say, "Oh, Long Gi-land," over-emphasizing the hard "G." I clearly said "Long Island," not, "Long Gi-land," but since there is a perception that all Long Islanders say it that way, Edith found it humorous to say that. The fact is, very few people say it that way. In fact I have very rarely heard it in all my years.

Maybe it would have been nice to know this couple years ago when a younger mind could have produced sharper humor. I clearly missed that opportunity. Take what you can get, is my motto.

Grant Suiter was the raison d'être for the Computer

Department. We had two System 38s in my half of the department (one "test" and one "production"), and I think at least one 370 mainframe in the Publishing Department. Maybe more, I don't know. Plus all the requisite refrigerator sized tape drives, washing machine sized DASD (Direct Access Storage Devices), and CRT terminals everywhere.

IBM was making plenty of money off of Watchtower.

One day a sort of celebration of the relationship between Watchtower and IBM was put on for the entire department. A bunch of IBM executives were there, and representing Watchtower were Grant Suiter, Ed Sainthill, Major Spry, and Verne Coffin. All in the department were invited.

The IBM execs spoke, and a skit was put on by Alice LaFranca and Jerry Hudson. Grant Suiter spoke about our great relationship with IBM, but couldn't help giving away the fact that the relationship will only continue to exist as long as it satisfies our need for ultimately supporting the main objective of Watchtower, which is the "dissemination of information." Since Watchtower plans on being in business at least as long if not longer than IBM and the rest of this "system of things," he was surreptitiously saying that, "We will have a relationship until we find a better way of doing things."

A few years later, Watchtower dumped the Publishing mainframe in favor of their own product, MEPS, but continued the Administrative Data (business) side of the house. Eventually, the System 38s also became dinosaurs.

Missed It By That Much

When we were getting to know Presley C, he told us about former GB member Ewart Chitty who had recently resigned that post with no explanation. Except to attempt to assure the family that it was not due to any misconduct or problems with the job. He apparently had simply decided that his service to God would be more effective without the complications associated with his former position.

Presley spoke of it as an educational, first-of-its-kind situation. In other words, positively.

Therefore I did not know Chitty as a GB member. But we were both Bethelites at the same time, from two years after his resignation until he was finally sent back to England, where he was from.

It might be that the real reason for Chitty's resignation and subsequent retention as a Brooklyn Bethel member for several years had to do with homosexual activity. Watchtower is so expert at hiding and/or spinning reality that it's nearly impossible to find information to confirm either the veracity or the falsehood of any claims that have been made. And, as was the case with Leo Greenlees, it is not the purpose of this tome to discuss history that is not connected with a story that I can tell first-hand. One can certainly do an internet search to find out anything I have found out that same way.

What I can confirm is that Chitty was a life-long single man that preferred young men as roommates, and that he formerly had a 30-year relationship with a male roommate. Also, he was thought by many, especially back in England where he was best known, to be a gay man.

It is interesting that he was not sent back to England until the final years of his life, an aged man with little to no means of support. He died in 1993 at the age of 95. His leaving Bethel has commonly been characterized as a dismissal, and there really is no other plausible explanation for it. To release an aged man from a volunteer job where his means of maintenance were always provided by the employer, to a life in another country where he would have to support himself completely, strongly suggests that some misconduct was involved. Add to that the fact that Watchtower always creates a smoking gun when such things happen with no explanation, which has the effect of almost assuring us that misconduct that they are not free to describe took place. As with Greenlees, speaking nothing about the case speaks volumes about the case.

Chitty was the interviewee on the first Family Night of my Bethel life. When asked why he never married, he said, "How can I pick one to marry? I love them all!"

I thought that was an odd thing to say. As it turns out, many women in the Bethel family felt it was more than odd. It gave them an undefinable "creepy" feeling.

Why? Because he could be talking about them in particular? Possibly making him a lecher? Or because he gave off a gay vibe, and it occurred to them that he was in fact gay? Maybe they felt that even subconsciously?

As was stated in Preserving the Sandbox, being gay is not a crime. Hiding that fact in an organization that condemns homosexual activity and administers severe discipline for it, all the while covering for a gay man who (theoretically) is gay, who existed at the highest level within the organization, is not criminal either. It is, however, immoral, misleading, hypocritical, and just plain wrong.

Raymond Franz had served on the GB for just under ten years when I arrived at Bethel. He had resigned the year before my arrival, but was still in "good standing" at that time.

While GB members were not "celebrities" in those days as they are today, many people in the organization had an idea of who Fred Franz was. And word was starting to get out about who his nephew Ray was. The Kingdom Ministry had already carried an announcement about a few Bethel staffers that had been dismissed and disfellowshipped for apostasy, and the fact of Ray's (so far benign) resignation was fairly well known.

From my arrival in autumn 1981 through the end of the year, aftershocks of the "apostates'" activity and subsequent dismissal were making for some ripe discussions among the Bethel family. In my experience, no one made the connection of that with anything about Ray. Yet.

There would be frequent talk about the "heaviness" that was felt until the apostates finally left. Everyone was glad to be rid of them. No sympathy or hopes of repentance and return to the organization were ever expressed. They were just evil people who might as well start burning in Gehenna now. And as nearly always happens when anyone is disfellowshipped, people expressed thoughts of being aware of tendencies among the apostates that they were now sure were incontrovertible evidence of their guilt, therefore the correctness of their punishment. I have never seen such disingenuous gloating in all of my life.

Meanwhile, people would voice concern for Ray, and ask how he was doing.

One day, the GB member who was chairman at Morning Worship finally answered the question. Essentially, it was reported that Ray was in Alabama, doing fine, and that there is no need for concern.

Then came the announcement that Ray had been disassociated. He had been seen dining with his landlord and employer, Peter Gregerson, who had disassociated himself. At the time of Ray's "offense," disassociated people were not to be treated the same as disfellowshipped people. The rule was changed AFTER Ray's alleged association with Gregerson, but BEFORE the announcement about him. There is probably no court in the world that will convict a man of breaking a law that was not in effect at the time of the "offense." Watchtower evidently operates under a different set of principles. Ray was gone as if by the wave of a magic wand, the way Watchtower wanted it.

They were sick of him, so they got rid of him without ever having to prove a thing about the real charges they had previously investigated to no avail.

It never occurred to us that there was anything amiss concerning the earlier table announcement that Ray was OK, and the fact that the events involving his eventual treatment were taking place at the same time. All one has to do is read the account of his and the other apostates' treatment in *Crisis of Conscience,* and one will see that the duplicity and hypocrisy of that announcement are quite palpable. We had been lied to. Not by Ray. By the Governing Body.

In February 1982, Time magazine published an article called *Witness Under Prosecution* with Ray's cooperation. In it he revealed anomalies about certain Watchtower teachings and practices. At the end of that article, it was said that the Witnesses "have necessarily backed off the 1975 date, but the End must occur during the lifetime of people who still remember the earthly events of 1914. With the rapidly thinning ranks of such oldsters, the Witnesses confront an increasingly troublesome, self-imposed and absolute deadline."

One day at work, Tim K and I were discussing the article. While I was no fan of Ray at the time, and was ever faithful to

Watchtower's eschatology, I felt compelled to say, "In a way he's right about one thing. Pretty soon we will face a troublesome, absolute deadline." Tim's response was, "That's no problem, they'll just change something, like the definition of 'generation,' or something."

As it turns out, both of us were right.

It wasn't until early 2018 that I finally decided to read *Crisis of Conscience.* I had been officially kicked out of the JW organization exactly two years prior, but I still maintained that they have the truth doctrinally, even if their procedures and treatment of people was sort of nutty. First of all, I no longer really had a reason to NOT read it. Secondly, I wanted and needed to prove to myself, once again, that JWs DO have the truth.

I will not discuss the book in great detail. I highly recommend you read it yourself if you haven't already. What I will comment on is its overall character, and the overall character of the author.

Ray had been so vilified by the entire organization, from the few at the top that knew the gory details, to those near but not at the top that were witnesses to some but not all things, to the millions who have no idea about the man, that there is nothing remotely positive that could be said about the man.

He must be the evil apostate with the "diseased mind" I was told about. The one who chooses to "beat his fellow slaves," his former brothers. The one who is just as bad as Judas Iscariot, who betrayed his Lord into death for 30 pieces of silver. The quintessential betrayer of God and Jesus themselves. The man with the most twisted, demented understanding of the scriptures in the history of Babylon the Great. The embodiment of Satan. The liar.

What I discovered was a man who had no bitterness in his heart toward his former brothers. Who never said one word that can be characterized as a personal attack on anyone.

Typical apostate literature that I had read in the past always contained unnecessary and nasty vitriol in the form of character assassination of Watchtower leaders, from CT Russell through the present day. It would contain no hope to replace the teachings held to be false. Just tearing down, no building up. Ugly attacks that went nowhere.

None of that is the case in Ray's writing.

All of the vilification I had heard from my Bethel associates and others had to be talking about another man. It was like describing a mouse as one might describe Godzilla.

Even my conversation with Carey Barber was now in question.

The Third Reich

Up to this point, I have reminisced about the fifteen Governing Body members that I have personally known through my days at Bethel: Carey Barber, Jack Barr, Lloyd Barry, John Booth, Fred Franz, George Gangas, Leo Greenlees, Milton Henschel, Ted Jaracz, Karl Klein, Martin Pötzinger, Albert Schroeder, Grant Suiter, Lyman Swingle, and Dan Sydlik. I have talked about three that preceded me, one of which I knew as a former GB member and two that I never knew, namely Ewart Chitty, and Raymond Franz and Nathan Knorr respectively. I have discussed one that I knew many years before his current membership on the GB, but did not serve with at Bethel, Sam Herd. And I have discussed a few other Bethel heavies that were not on the GB.

The only other member of the current GB that I know personally is Gerrit Lösch. But I will also make some brief comments about several other modern day members whom I almost feel that I know through other people, mainly Bethel family members who were in my congregation up until ten years ago, and two relatives of one GB member.

Gerrit Lösch had been invited to serve at Brooklyn Bethel in 1990. Sometime in late spring/early summer of 1994, one of the well-connected Watchtower Farms Bethelites in our congregation in Sussex, Keith F, booked him for a Public Talk that autumn. By the time that date arrived, Lösch had been appointed to the Governing Body.

Keith asked if Lösch and his wife, Merete, could stay with us at our three bedroom home with a full basement that served as a family/music room or an extra bedroom with a private bathroom. We gladly accepted.

The Lösches arrived early that weekend.

I was well aware of Lösch's former position as overseer of the Austrian branch. There he also oversaw the work in East Germany and other countries that were under the tentacles of the USSR. Therefore he had intimate knowledge of the Stasi and the KGB, the infiltration of the congregations by agents of those bodies, and the significant trials that caused.

While in the field service with them, I had some alone time with Gerrit in the car. For years I had experienced intense stress over behaviors within my elder body in Sussex. In particular, I wanted to talk to him about the way decisions were made and carried out.

Regardless of the discussion at elders meetings, and the decisions arrived at, things would almost always be carried out the way a certain elder wanted them to be. Many day-to-day decisions excluded input from elders that he knew would not agree with him. One of the results was that I would often hear about certain decisions from just about any member of the congregation, never having been included in or informed about the discussion. The elder in question was nothing more than a big bully who played cheap emotional games with everyone to get his way and curry favor. Abuses by him and other elders went much farther than already described, but I really just wanted to get Lösch's opinion on the dysfunctionality of the elder body that started with the bully.

Lösch made a forceful gesture with his clenched right hand and said, "You have to get in there and tell them what is right. Be strong about it."

"I think I've tried that. A circuit overseer recommended that, as Secretary, I should document all decisions, get the entire body to sign those minutes, and hold them to them."

"And did you do that?"

"Yes, and I got into trouble for it. I was eventually removed as Secretary. Then it got REALLY ugly."

The conversation ended there when the other two in our group returned to the car. I thought it would come up again sometime during the weekend. It didn't. If Lösch wanted to, he would have brought it up again. He did not. Just as it happened with the CO, I felt hung out to dry. Abandoned.

One of the things that endeared Lösch to me and others was his love of nature. Well into the evening that Saturday, he took me out to my front porch and pointed out some of the constellations and other formations in the night sky. In particular I remember him pointing out Cassiopeia and the Milky Way. I have spent too little time in my life observing such awesomeness. I appreciated him showing me what he did.

Earlier that same day, while we were sitting on my backyard deck, he allowed a wasp to land on his forefinger. He looked at the wasp, holding his hand still, then turning it for everyone to see while he marveled at the wasp's beauty. The fact is, I hate wasps. They have an evil look to them, and their sting hurts like hell. When I was still a toddler, I once licked a lollipop that a wasp had gotten stuck to. I was too young to remember it, but my Mom recalls my pained screeches like it was yesterday.

Yeah, I hate wasps. But the WASP that was demonstrating the beauty of creation made it more than OK.

At some point, Lösch fetched a push broom from my garage and swept all of the autumn leaves off of my deck. No announcement, he just did it.

Two strange observations about Lösch: He has recommended to single Bethelites, young men who room together, that they kneel beside their bed, hold hands, and pray together before retiring for the night. And he has been very vocal about his hatred for American football, saying that no one should watch it. I'm not sure how well either of those ideas went over with the Bethel family in general.

Being that we were in a congregation with Bethelites from Watchtower Farms, we would frequently hear about things GB members have said or done, accompanied by absurd praise. When they published a new songbook around 2010, all credit was given to GB member David Splane, as if he is some sort of musical genius. Of course, since the songbook is yet another "gift from Jehovah." it must be that Splane is also a sort of gift from above for having been a chief architect of what Jehovah gave us. Or something like that.

I have never liked any of the songbooks, but the 2010 version was a new and all-time low for several reasons.

The music is emotionless. In that entire book, there are less than a handful of songs with musical slurs (where two or more notes of different pitches are played in succession without a break). That alone makes that collection the stiffest, most cardboard music in history. Also, nearly every syllable of every word in the entire book is assigned one and only one beat/note. Again, no possibility of musical expression or beauty. Adding to that, the words are nearly always awkward and unsingable.

One may argue that the beauty is in the meaning of the words. But that is only one small part of good music. There is also the sound of the words, the timing and expressivity of the words, and of course the music itself.

About all I know about Splane is that he is a very stiff, uninteresting speaker. And that, if he is actually the author or even the editor of that songbook, he should stop doing things like that. Don't even try taking music lessons of any kind. Just stop. Please.

The Khalil family were very dear friends of ours in Westbury. The father, Fayez is a beautiful soul. He and his lovely wife Ida produced three precious girls, all close in age, and a much younger son. Their middle daughter, Magda married a Bethelite named Richard Souang. They remained at Bethel together. Richard's step-father is former GB member Guy Pierce, who served until his death in 2014. That is literally all I know about Guy Pierce, having never met the man.

I know even less about five other current GB members Geoffrey Jackson, Mark Sanderson, Kenneth Cook Jr, Gage Fleegle, and Jeffrey Winder. That is to say, I know NOTHING about them. Except that I saw Jackson's testimony before the Australian Royal Commission, the same as anyone who has access to YouTube may. Painful to watch. A GB member who is merely a "consultant," who is not involved in decision making. Yikes. The Oxford English Dictionary and Merriam Webster should have a picture of Jackson next to the definition of "disingenuous." Or maybe next to a different word, a four letter word that starts with "L" and ends with "R," with "IA" in the middle.

"You would love our Circuit Overseer. He has the most comical face. He makes expressions like..." Bill C and his wife demonstrated the way rubber-faced Stephen Lett uses his visage to make a point.

I thought they had to be exaggerating. But anyone that has seen Lett speak on the JW website knows that it is impossible to exaggerate about the phenomenon.

Bill and his wife were not poking fun at Lett. They truly love and respect the man, as they would any JW representative.

In 1999, Lett was appointed to the GB.

This writer has never met Lett or seen him speak in person.

Only on the JW website and YouTube videos. Every one of those viewing experiences has created a state of utter amazement. Not the good kind of amazement. The other kind.

Many examples could be cited; two should suffice.

It is just remarkable, in fact staggering, that he has seized upon COVID-19 as the sole piece of evidence that, "We are living in the final part of the last days, undoubtedly the final part of the final part of the last days, shortly before the last day of the last days."

Golly gee, that's lotsa "final parts," and even more lotsa "last days." So very clever. Must be true.

It used to be that the emphasis was on the progressive and composite nature of the sign of the last days. Apparently now it's just about whatever single factor is dominating the news, and whatever will convince an emotionally driven adherent (READ: fearful) to keep on waiting with blinders on. Oh well.

The second instance of amazing oratory by Lett is his famous speech wherein he speaks of "apostate-driven lies" (a new term coined by Watchtower) when refuting the well documented fact that "[Jehovah's organization] is permissible toward pedophiles." He then comically goes on to state that, "If anybody takes action against someone who has threatened our young ones, and takes action to protect our young ones, its Jehovah's organization." Okay, Steve, anything you say.

I feel like I know Anthony Morris, even though we have never met and I've never seen him speak in person. Again only on the JW website and YouTube videos.

I feel that way because so many of the things he has said have absolutely astounded me, and I often brought them up with Sussex elders from Watchtower Farms. Their defense of him has made it seem that he was standing right behind them, prodding them to obediently defend the indefensible. Just one example should explain the astonishment he so often engenders.[4]

---

4 On February 22, 2023, shortly before this book went into final production, it was announced at JW World Headquarters that Anthony Morris is no longer serving as a member of the Governing Body.

The GB had recently informed the congregations that the Book Study was being discontinued, primarily due to gasoline prices in certain parts of the world. Eventually they came up with Family Worship as a replacement. And eventually it was spun as if that was the plan along.

Left out of this new "blessing from Jehovah" were single people, but more importantly people with so much opposition at home that Family Worship is an impossibility. In particular, there were women in my and other congregations whose husbands would not allow a Bible or any other literature in their home, and would not allow their wives to instruct the children about their beliefs. That may seem extreme, but it is very often a reality. It is not difficult to imagine less severe circumstances also putting the Family Worship arrangement out of reach for many.

So I was in a state of disbelief when I heard Morris say to a large audience, "Anyone who is not taking full advantage of Family Worship will not be prepared for Armageddon."

Does Morris have any idea of the massive discouragement that thoughtless statement made for many, especially women with kids and opposed husbands? How utterly hopeless he made good people feel whose every day is a serious struggle? After all they've been through, are going through, and will go through, they won't be "prepared for Armageddon" anyway? This from a respected leader?

Unfortunately, outrageously ill-advised, hurtful statements from that source are the norm.

Time to Go

After spending several years on various projects in the Administrative Data half of the Computer Department, I was finally assigned to be the project manager of a new Mortgage and Insurance system for Lyman Swingle's Treasurer's Office. I had worked on Cost Accounting applications, General Ledger, a brand new Order Entry and Inventory system, and the Accounts Payable system. I had done one-off programs such as one that produced a report of all of the Watchtower investment holdings (apart from real estate, there wasn't much to write home about – mainly very conservative bank accounts and government bonds). Being the only resource in the department that had a working knowledge of various municipalities in the greater New York City area, I produced an elaborate report on Watchtower's business dealings with companies in that vicinity. That report would serve to convince the mayor and the five borough presidents (Planning Commission) that Watchtower spent enough money locally to make what would eventually become the 90 Sands building worth their approval. And there was that little report for Lloyd Barry already mentioned.

The new Mortgage and Insurance system would replace the old one that had significant functional deficiencies. I worked closely with Judah Schroeder and a fellow named Roger to develop all of the business and functional specifications for the new system. By the time the project entered the coding phase, a major change occurred for me.

My wife had been feeling ill far more frequently than normal. We were both concerned, but not overly so, being that we were too young to have experienced significant health issues, hence naïve to the possibilities. One morning, she called me about the results of her medical appointment with Dr. Dixon.

She was pregnant.

I was thrilled. She was thrilled that I was thrilled.

The first time we would actually see each other after learning that news would be at lunch in the 4th dining room, at the table of Don and Dee Adams. We both sported shit-eating grins and left everyone at the table in the dark for the time being.

We had actually discussed having children while still living in Westbury, before our application to Bethel, but put those thoughts on hold. Now the discussion was no longer, "Should we have a baby," but consisted of all the questions any soon-to-be new parents need to discuss. With the addition of the question of where we would live, since we would have to leave Bethel to start this new lifestyle.

I wasn't sorry to leave Bethel. Up until my selection as the project manager for Mortgages and Insurance, I had increasingly felt that I was viewed with suspicion, mainly because I had exposed some serious security flaws in the IBM System 38 that the Watchtower people were convinced did not exist. They were so proud and boastful of that computer that one would swear they were the designers and manufacturers of it. It was actually very strange how they defended its properties in the face of scrutiny. You'd think they would appreciate learning of any system flaws they should be aware of, but they acted as if I had CREATED the flaws, rather than EXPOSED them. And as if the S38 were another provision from Jehovah, hence criticism of it was tantamount to criticism of the organization. Very strange indeed.

For that and other reasons, I had grown quite unhappy at Bethel. Oh I still loved the fact that we were in the international hub, the center of all the action. But what came with that were excessive rules, an unrelenting schedule, an assignment to an inexplicably ice-cold congregation, and poverty, among other things. My trouble was, I viewed it as the ultimate assignment (with the possible exception of Gilead missionary service), therefore anything I did after that would be letting the Creator of the universe down. So thoughts of leaving versus staying created profound conflict within me. My wife felt similarly, but was more willing to accept whatever may happen. I recall discussing it with Monroe F during a card game at his home in Westbury. I had the utmost respect for Monroe. He was not a Bethel man, so his views were non-biased. Still, we didn't come to any conclusion.

Now that the decision had been made for us, we chose to dwell on the joy of bringing a new life into the world.

We knew where we would live. The young family that was occupying the apartment in the upstairs of my in-laws house in Hicksville, Long Island would be moving out just at the right time, so that was taken care of, at a slightly discounted rate. My father would later sell us his Datsun 810 for cheap. All I needed was a job.

And I needed to leave the Mortgage and Insurance system in a completed state before I left.

My main assistant, Jack P was a very liable and talented resource. He did most of the coding and testing, especially during my frequent absences spent on job interviews. I had to leave just short of implementation, but that phase would be in Jack's good hands.

Before we left, I recall Don Adams cheerfully telling us that springtime was a great time to be leaving Bethel and setting up a new home with a new family. I very much appreciated his positive spirit. Don and Dee subsequently visited us for weekends a few times at our new home in Hicksville, and when we later moved to Hamburg New Jersey.

While we were no longer intimately associated with GB members, we maintained contact with many Bethel friends. They visited us often and we visited them on occasion. When our congregation in Sussex New Jersey finally became a Watchtower Farms Bethel congregation, we were back to constantly hearing Bethel news as well as visiting the Farm, especially for entire weekends with our new friends Curtis and Dawn Carpenter and others.

My final years in Sussex were also part of my final years as one of Jehovah's Witnesses.

After I had finally stepped down from an appointed position once and for all, I began seeing things more from the outside looking in. I observed things at the meetings that I still went to faithfully that made me realize that the various anomalies I had observed and experienced over the years were not accidental – they were deliberate. The virtual worship of the elders and the GB was not a local phenomenon peculiar to certain groups and congregations – it was actually being taught in the pages of the Watchtower. For example, articles about elders and their duties would discuss, not what things would be like IF the elders did what they're supposed to do, but as thing supposedly ARE since the elders are so incredibly wonderful.

I became increasingly shocked at the bizarre things routinely said by the GB and its representatives, especially from the mouths of Anthony Morris and Stephen Lett. Just a small sample of those things have already been mentioned in the chapter The Third Reich.

I started to see the GB as taking the place of God himself.

Family Worship night was described simultaneously as a gift from Jehovah, and a gift from the Governing Body. Especially since all it is is a suggestion on how to spend an evening, it's an extreme over-reach to give credit to a group of men for it. As if they designed the solar system with the earth's rotation and revolution around the sun. Congregants would routinely say things like, "Isn't it loving for the Governing Body to provide us with a new evening for Family Worship." Nobody would ever correct that inanity.

The new songbook was also a provision of not just Jehovah, but the Governing Body.

The Governing Body all of a sudden became synonymous with the Faithful and Discreet Slave.[5]

They even unilaterally invented a new definition for the word "generation," one that does not exist in any dictionary (Bible or common) in any language in any culture in the history of mankind, claiming that this is the definition of "generation" as used in the Bible.

It wasn't for those reasons that I left the organization. They were just the tip of the iceberg that motivated me to finally do

---

5   Interesting, since that slave was supposedly appointed by Jesus himself in 1919, and the GB didn't actually come into existence as such until 52 years later, in 1971. Before that, the board of directors performed purely business duties, nothing of a spiritual nature. The only use of the expression "governing body" in the publications before 1971 was one reference made in the 1940s to all of the corporate members, which numbered in the hundreds of people spread all over the map, very few if any serving at Bethel headquarters. Again, not a body that as a whole supervises anything, or anyone, or that dispenses "spiritual food."

research to prove to myself that Jehovah's Witnesses DO have the truth. That research only turned up flaw after flaw, to the point that I finally realized how wild an assumption it is to say that they do have "the truth."

Fun Facts

At some point, when the GB was up to 18 men in size, a table was procured for their meeting room that would fit all of them comfortably.

In those days, most if not all of the office furniture was donated by various companies to Watchtower. Whether it was too old for the original owners, or they just wanted to redecorate, much of the furniture was still in very good condition, and the company would of course get a tax deduction for donating to a charitable organization. I believe much of the furniture procured for the 25 Columbia Heights office building[6] was from Citibank. Including that huge globe that was situated just next to the revolving doors of the entrance on Vine Street, and was repainted over the course of many weeks by one of the artists in the Art Department.

---

6   Watchtower had purchased the Squibb Pharmaceuticals complex in 1969. Remodeling was completed and the facility dedicated in 1982. What became 30 Columbia Heights had offices and other facilities, such as shipping, Gilead school, Braille manufacturing, and tape duplicating. 25 Columbia Heights was all offices. Computer Department was one of the first departments to move into the 25 building, occupying the 5th and 6th floors. That move-in was completed just before our arrival in autumn 1981.

The GB meeting table in the 10th floor Executive office had a huge hole in the middle that was similar in shape to the table itself. A common joke among the Bethelites was that that is where the Shekinah light shone when they communicated with the guy upstairs. The fact is, it was just that way when it arrived from Citibank, and was probably the only table suitable for its purpose.

The table was soon replaced by a solid one without a hole, not because of the jokes being circulated, but because, as Don Adams explained to me, "They need to be able to pass papers back and forth across the table, so they need a table without a hole in the middle." The new table was probably built in the Bethel carpentry shop.

Fred Franz played the harmonica. I once asked him to do a Family Night bit with me, but his response was only a blank downward stare at the table.

Dan Sydlik was 51 years old when he married 23-year-old

Marina Hodson in 1970. There is a difference of 28 years between them. They were a very much loved couple.

The 1986 wedding ceremony of Judah Ben Schroeder and Amber Baker, took place at Bethel's 107 Columbia Heights Kingdom Hall. However, the reception took place on a yacht in New York Harbor. All GB members attended except two, according to my recollection. One of the two non-attenders was George Gangas. I'm not sure about the other one, or if there was also a third one. Word among the family was that they didn't want all of the GB on a boat in a harbor, either so that someone would be at headquarters if needed, or in case an accident occurred that could wipe out the GB, or both.

Word was also that many were taken aback by the opulence of this extremely expensive event, which included a life-sized photographic poster of Amber positioned at the entrance of the Kingdom Hall. I didn't know and still don't know Amber, but I did know Judah and thought very highly of him. How the father, Dale Baker chose to spend his money, especially on his daughter and new son-in-law, was his business. If it were my money and my daughter I might do the same. Well, probably not, but theoretically I might.

Not the actual Governing Body table, but an idea of what it was like in the late-1970s to early-1980s.

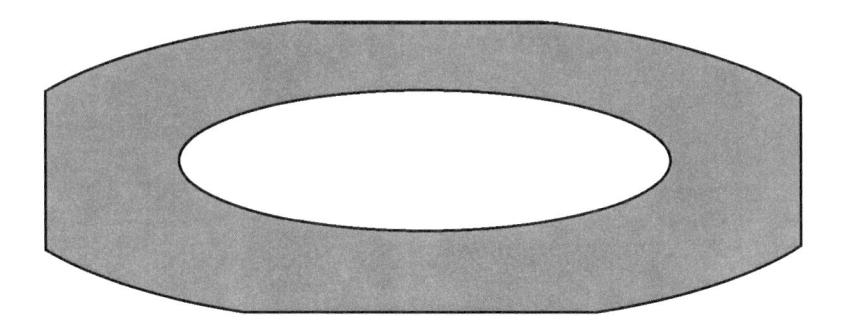

Crude birds-eye view drawing closer to the actual shape of that same table.

Why

The purpose of this book is not to convince anyone of the Watchtower's position in the world, whether that be a true or false prophet, a true or false religion, just a publishing business, a cult, or any other kind of entity one might conjure. The writer has his opinion about such things, and the readers will have their own as well.

Neither is its purpose to discuss doctrines or convince anyone of a particular interpretation.

Nor to convince anyone that they should have a certain opinion about certain people or bodies of people.

Nor to encourage hatred or resentment toward men the reader might see as having lied to them, misled them, and prevented them from having a normal life.

Its purpose is to show, from personal experience, the human side of men who exist(ed) in the ether of Watchtower, out of reach of most of the people they have affected. That human side is, as with all humans, sometimes laudable, sometimes despicable. And everything in between.

Since Jehovah's Witnesses are generally taught a version of "learned helplessness," they are dependent upon their authority figures to tell them what is right and wrong, how to think, how to behave. Therefore, post-JWs often tend to exist in a victim state, blaming their failures and difficult feelings on the organization, its Governing Body, and its elder bodies.

For a person to make true and healthy progress, it is absolutely essential to grow beyond that tendency to blame others for their problems and difficulties.

Seeing the humanity of the Watchtower brass has hopefully helped all to see that there is good and bad in even those people at the top.

It's easy to stop blaming a given individual if we now see them as essentially a good, albeit misguided person. It's not as easy to stop blaming a given individual who has truly and deliberately done bad things, for example not just blindly supporting the protection Watchtower affords pedophiles, but actually engineering and facilitating the mechanisms responsible for that protection. Our hearts naturally go out to victims of such institutional abuse. For them it understandably is especially difficult to forgive and forget. Still, it is always possible and necessary to move past the blame phase and make something of one's life.

Seeing the humanity involved should also help us to see how the trauma experienced by many has been created, not just by the religion itself, but by localized attitudes and interpretations of the rules that have caused or contributed to that trauma. As mentioned in this book's preface, once we have a better identification of what has caused the trauma, we are better equipped to deal with it. Put another way, how are we to deal with trauma if we never have an accurate understanding of what really happened, of what or who caused it? That doesn't necessarily mean we need to know and dwell on all of the gory details, but at least we can have a correct understanding of the details we do know.

Whether we are a recovered or recovering post-JW, the possibilities for us are now endless. We are no longer defined by a narrow set of rules, including the absurd notion that so-called "independent thinking," (a cultic expression if ever there was one), will get us in trouble. Since we're no longer responsible to the controllers within Watchtower, but are mainly responsible to ourselves, it is not really logical to continually blame anyone outside of ourselves for our situation. If we are in control, we are responsible. If we are responsible, we are in control. It may seem more desirable to be in control WITHOUT being responsible, but we can't have one without the other.

We are free.

GLOSSARY

Bethel:

Any branch office of the JWs anywhere in the world, where donations are used to make books and stuff dirt cheap with (almost) free labor.

Bethelite:

Someone who lives at Bethel and provides the free labor.

Bethel Family:

All of the Bethelites at a given branch. A very big family of people who are mostly unrelated to each other and in fact don't know who most of the other members are. Except for the ones that are on TV a lot. Not really a family.

(Bethel) Family Night:

An evening of entertainment put on by Bethelites for the Bethel family. Features skits, musical numbers, and interviews. Also includes Chippendale dancers, but only in the minds of those who are bored and horny.

(Bethel) Family Watchtower Study:

An hour every Monday night spent rehashing a Watchtower study article that was already read, and then studied, and will then be gone over for the fourth time at the congregation

Watchtower study. In other words, a great way to fritter away a Monday evening.

Body of Elders:

A group of men in each congregation that are imperfect as individuals, but somehow become perfect as a body. They are not paid for their work. Rather they support themselves and their families variously as plumbers, shoe salesmen, car mechanics, truck drivers etc. Their skills include fixing toilets, selling shoes, changing motor oil, driving trucks, etc. They occasionally receive specialized training designed to convince everyone they have been trained.

Circuit:

A group of usually twelve to sixteen congregations in geographic proximity that are organized for maximum control. Cuz why not?

Circuit Assembly:

A weekend meeting of a circuit, or half of a circuit, wherein insomnia is temporarily relieved without opiates. There is usually a pool for people who want to pledge their eternal allegiance to the organization by getting wet.

Circuit Overseer:

A traveling elder who oversees a circuit of congregations. One of his main functions is to bill the congregations for his groceries, dry cleaning, and car and other expenses after eating free meals from Tuesday through Sunday elaborately prepared by women in the congregation, cleaning the same suits that were just cleaned recently, and riding in other people's cars without contributing for gasoline. If he is married, his wife tags along for congregation visits, but humbly keeps her mouth shut due to her being born female. She may at times share her opinion with other females only, as long as it's kept to fashion choices, nifty fried chicken recipes, and how to thread a sewing needle without drawing blood.

District Convention (Assembly):
A usually three-day event that uses the same (mis)information every year but with a different stimulatingly clever name. All of the talks, demonstrations and interviews conform to the convention name, but are otherwise recycled twaddle designed to put to sleep the insomniacs that the Circuit Assembly missed. Typical names are *One More Year To Go* (1974), *Frozen Orange Juice* (1981), *Generation According to Us* (2008), *Jesus Creates the GB in 1971, Then Appoints it in 1919, or Dr Brown's Triumphant Flux Capacitor* (2013), and *Australian Royal What?* (2017). Has a bigger pool than the circuit assembly. More wetness, but no swimming.

District Overseer:
A traveling elder who overseers a litter of circuit overseers. One of his main functions is to bill the entire circuit for expenses similar to that of the circuit overseer, after tag-teaming with him to use the same resources for free. Like the circuit overseer, he may also be married. If so, his wife will behave identically to the circuit overseer's wives, setting a superb example of subjugation... er, subjection.

Entrants School:

A school for new Bethelites that takes up one evening per week for about a half year. A trusty way of adjusting to the fact that they will have virtually no free time as long as they stay at The House of Gawd. Among things learned are how to spell Mesopotamia, how to tell the difference between a pizza and a snood, and sculpting with bat guano.

Factory Dispatch:

The act of killing a factory. Quickly.

Family Worship Night:

A gift from the Governing Body of an extra night for all JWs to study with their families at home. Not in addition to the seven we all have already. Just an extra night. Or maybe it is an eighth night. Kind of hard to explain. Never mind...

Generation:

This word's definition changes periodically, according to the amount of time between 1914 CE and the current year. *Do not, under any circumstances, consult a dictionary, as it will just lead to confusion*. As of this writing, generation now means "two generations that overlap." By about 2035, that will change to "THREE generations that overlap," (since Exodus mentions not two, but three). By about 2095, that will change to "a whole big mess of lots a people who saw neat stuff and are super-patient and just really great, obedient folks." Some time after that, it will permanently change to, "one more question and you're disfellowshipped."

Gilead School:

A school that trains two classes of students every year for worldwide missionary work. Excludes individual learning specific to various country assignments, such as language, adapting to local customs, and how to NOT have sex without getting pregnant.

Governing Body:

The body of "anointed" older men who oversee the entire segment of the world that is not "worldly." Or according to GB member Jackson, a random bunch of consultants who don't know what the hell is going on and take no responsibility for anything. Or according to GB member Lösch, a group of men who take up space and don't answer to Watchtower in any way. The Governing Body was what Jesus was actually talking about when he discussed the Faithful and Discreet Slave. He just didn't know that until it was decided in 2013 by none other than the Governing Body.

Jack Barr:

Two tools for changing a car tire.

John Booth:

A bathroom stall.

Kerfuffle:

A word that was not used in this book. Oh well, you can't have everything.

Kingdom Hall:

The main meeting place of all JWs. Their chief location for

learning "present truth," as opposed to truth. There are no icons or religious images used in these places of worship. Instead, all worship goes directly to the elders and the Governing Body.

Morning Worship:

A 7:00 AM meeting of the entire Bethel family wherein everyone is forced to listen to a chairman and four other people expound upon a single paragraph for about twenty minutes. All must also stare at pots of coffee that may not be touched until after the prayer that ends the charade. Then, along with the coffee, breakfast is consumed, consisting of food that ranges from excellent to suitable only for coyotes.

SEX:

If you don't already know, I can't help you...

Section Men:

The guys in the Service Department that oversee traveling elders in various states in the USA, or guys that are serious about the proper way to eat grapefruit.

INDEX

Adams, Don....................................46, 58, 109, 201, 204, 209
Administrative Data (Department)..........47, 106, 154, 178, 200
Administrative Data Committee (ADC)...................36, 106, 151
Art Department..104, 208
Aulicino, Ciro...40, 41, 84, 94
Australian Royal Commission...133, 194
Backmasking...98, 101, 103, 105
Baker, Dale..210
Barber, Carey 154, 156, 157, 158, 159, 160, 161, 162, 163, 164, 165, 166, 169, 187
Barber, Sydney...154, 159, 162, 163
Barr, Jack..141, 142, 143
Barr, Mildred..142, 144
Barry, Lloyd.........................29, 128, 130, 132, 134, 200
Bedford Stuyvesant, New York...95, 96
Bestiality at Watchtower Farms..78
Bethel Office..71, 72, 101, 122
Booth, John..60, 61, 145, 146
Brooklyn Heights, New York.......10, 70, 86, 113, 159, 160, 165
Butler, Bob...134
Campbell, Merton...84
Chapman, Percy...60
Chitty, Ewart...179, 180, 181
Chyke, Calvin................................134, 135, 136, 137, 138, 139
Chyke, Zelda...135, 136
Coffin, Verne..177
Columbus Circle, New York..135, 143
Computer Department..41, 42, 47, 86, 106, 153, 154, 176, 200, 208
Cost Accounting Department................................48, 125, 200
Couch, George...31, 99, 100
Crisis of Conscience....................................150, 165, 184, 185
Dies, Harold..48, 125, 126
Dixon, Dr Lowell..116, 201
Doosenberry, Ray & Jean...57
Dwelling Together in Unity..78
E.T. The Extra Terrestrial..51, 55, 148

Eliot, Lisa..26
Factory Dispatch...134, 135
Family Night. .41, 84, 85, 86, 87, 89, 90, 92, 93, 118, 120, 126, 146, 181, 209
Family Night Committee..............................40, 84, 91
Family Watchtower study...........................72, 74, 99, 101, 156
Family Worship...198, 205, 206
Franz, Fred.....61, 106, 107, 108, 109, 110, 111, 123, 152, 182, 209
Franz, Raymond...4, 62, 63, 141, 150, 154, 161, 165, 166, 167, 169, 170, 182, 183, 184, 185, 186
Friend, Sam..43
Gangas, George....60, 61, 64, 65, 67, 68, 69, 70, 71, 72, 73, 93, 123, 210
Garza, Pat..132
Glen Cove, New York..................................94, 95, 96
Greenlees, Leo...................44, 59, 60, 61, 62, 63, 124, 133, 180
Greenpoint, New York...44
Gregerson, Peter..183
Hanagami, Ricky..89
Henschel, Milton...152, 153
Herd, Samuel................................20, 21, 22, 23, 24, 25, 26, 27
Hicksville, New York.......................17, 58, 203, 204
Hunkins, Bill..135
IBM...41, 42, 177, 202
Indexing Department..155
Jackson, Geoffrey..194
Jaracz (Lasko), Melita...29, 30
Jaracz, Theodore......28, 29, 30, 84, 93, 127, 128, 130, 132, 133
Klein, Karl..89, 104, 105, 118, 119, 120
Knorr, Nathan.29, 30, 57, 58, 78, 109, 117, 121, 122, 124, 128, 132, 152
LaFranca, Alice.......................................104, 105, 177
LaFranca, Pat..104
Larson, Max...134, 173
Legal Department...151
Lett, Stephen...195, 196, 205
Long Island, New York............10, 30, 58, 65, 94, 159, 176, 203
Lösch, Gerrit..188, 189, 190, 191, 192
Malawi...32, 33
Marcy, Victor..122

MEPS..41, 178
Mexico..32, 100
Miller, Harley..28
Morning Worship.....46, 51, 59, 61, 68, 91, 103, 110, 117, 145, 148, 149, 150, 154, 171, 183
Morris, Anthony...103, 197, 198, 205
Mr. Coffee...172, 173
Murray Hill, New York...69
Opening Up (hazing)..113, 114, 115, 116
Personnel Committee..145
Personnel Department..40, 42
Pierce, Guy...194
Pötzinger, Gertrude.......................................70, 147, 148, 150
Pötzinger, Martin....................................70, 147, 148, 149, 150
Return of the Jedi..148
Room bids..121, 122, 123
Russell, Charles Taze..46, 186
Rutherford, Joseph Franklin..120
Saint Jean, Michael...84, 91, 92
Sainthill, Ed...41, 42, 43, 177
Salih, Natheer...111, 112
Schroeder (Baker), Amber..210
Schroeder, Albert.................................47, 48, 50, 51, 53, 54, 56
Schroeder, Judah Ben.........................47, 48, 151, 201, 210
Service Committee..127, 167, 168
Service Department..............28, 91, 95, 127, 130, 131, 167, 168
Snail, Stanley...84
Songer, Dean...93, 126
Splane, David..192, 193
Spry, Major..177
Suiter, Edith..124, 171, 173, 175, 176
Suiter, Grant...31, 35, 36, 38, 39, 106, 124, 149, 166, 171, 172, 173, 174, 175, 176, 177
Sussex, New Jersey..65, 112, 158, 160, 164, 165, 189, 197, 204
Swingle, Crystal..150
Swingle, Lyman...150, 151, 152, 200
Sydlik (Hodson), Marina..82, 124, 210
Sydlik, Daniel...40, 41, 42, 44, 81, 84, 86, 87, 95, 96, 115, 124, 209
Time article "Witness Under Prosecution"............................184
Treasurer's Office............................42, 47, 48, 106, 172, 200

Trump, Donald..151
Underwood, Don..135
Wallen, Robert..32
WatchText..41
Watchtower Farms...........................41, 77, 189, 192, 197, 204
Westbury, New York....9, 10, 16, 28, 30, 31, 34, 35, 37, 87, 94, 106, 194, 201, 203
Wheelock, Richard..134, 173
Wisegarver, Vernon..151
Woody, Joy..48
Worsley, Arthur..57, 58
Writing Committee...128
Writing Department.....................38, 39, 40, 94, 128, 130, 131
Zulo, Mario..173